An Introduction to Business Law in the Middle East

An Introduction to Business Law in the Middle East

Edited by

Brian Russell

DRAKE PUBLISHERS INC.

NEW YORK · LONDON

Published in 1976 by
Drake Publishers, Inc.,
801 Second Avenue
New York, N. Y. 10017

Library of Congress Cataloging in Publication Data: 76-16362
Main entry under title:

An Introduction to business law in the Middle East.

Selected papers from a conference entitled Business law in the Middle East, held in London, May 14, 1975, and organized by Legal Studies and Services Limited.
1. Commercial law -- Near East -- Congresses. 2. Taxation -- Near East -- Law -- Congresses. I. Russell, Brian. II. Legal Studies and Services Limited.
Law 346.07'0956 76-16362
ISBN 0-8473-1254-2

Printed in the United States of America.

Preface

It is usually much easier to obtain the right answer than to discover whether you have asked the right question. A mistake resulting from the latter is also likely to be much more expensive. The purpose of this book is to ensure that the reader will become aware of some of the many questions that are likely to arise and the pitfalls he risks encountering when he starts to trade in, or with, the countries of the Middle East.

The contents of the book are based on the papers delivered at the conference 'Business Law in the Middle East' held in London on May 14, 1975 and organized by Legal Studies and Services Limited, Ramillies Buildings, Hills Place, London W1. This was probably the first conference in the world to specialise in the commercial law of so many Middle Eastern countries; it was certainly the first in the United Kingdom. We were therefore treading new ground and it was felt that the theme should be strictly practical, to give the requirements and back-ground of the region and its business atmosphere, rather than an exhaustive comparative study. This book adopts the same, practical approach and to this end, a list of company income tax rates and a chart highlighting the dey factors in industrial property, trade and investment have been compiled and reproduced as Appendices.

David Suratgar's contribution opens the book and provides an informed and personal conspectus of the form of the Law of Islam and how it has been altered in practice by the reformist movement and the pressure of new economic growth. This is followed by the contribution of Jamal Nasir which underlines, in very practical terms, the requirements for successful negotiation. Julian Lee's views upon taxation and tax planning, which (like other virtuous occupations) should begin at home, should prove most beneficial when the initial stages of entry into the area are under consideration. Thereafter Nigel Spinks provides guidance as to the practical aspects of actually doing business in the area and Sami El-Falahi discusses the legal environment for negotiating commercial agreements. Finally, Vivian Brown indicates the British Government's thoughts on how it may best help its exporters and businessmen.

A helpful feature of the book is that each contribution is followed by some of the questions put to each speaker by the delegates attending the original conference and the answers they received to them.

The countries discussed are all oil-producers. They are faced with and are surmounting successfully in a most remarkable way, the problems of vastly increased wealth and influence that have come, almost in the twinkling of an eye, not once, but twice. It is easy to forget in these post-1973 days that their initial surge of wealth came with the advent of the '50 - 50' petroleum concessions some twenty years ago. The area has been, and is being, transformed from one of major economic power, with the ability to cause recessions in world trade whenever it should please. However the traditions and precepts of the Koran and the binding effect of Islam should ensure that this new power is used wisely in the world as well as in those countries that are the subject of this study.

Brian Russell,
Gray's Inn,
London, W.C.1.

November, 1975

It should be noted that the value of the British £ against various middle eastern currencies in May 1975 should be adjusted to reflect current levels.

Contents

An Introduction to Business Law in the Middle East

The Development of the Legal Systems of the Middle East; Islamic Law and the Importance of Civil Law to the Process of Modernisation

by

David Suratgar

David Suratgar, besides being a Director of Morgan Grenfell & Co. Ltd., is also a Senior Fellow in the Institute of International and Foreign Trade Law at the Georgetown University School of Law, Washington D.C.

1—Introduction

So far as the Western world is concerned, London has been for a century the main centre for the study of the law of the Middle East, with its institutions like the Institute of Advanced Legal Studies and the School of Oriental and African Studies at London University and the work of scholars such as Professor Shacht and Sir Norman Anderson. This chapter, it should be noted draws heavily from the works of these two eminent scholars and the writer would like to express his debt to them.

So far as the United States is concerned, interest in the law of the Middle East is considerable, but much more recent. There are several centres of this work, but particular mention should be made of the Middle East Institute in Washington. The main professors and researchers have been people like Professor Khedouri, Professor Liebesny and Dr. Saba Habachy who have been teaching experimental courses during the last few years.

The other principal source of interest in the law of this area has probably come from the lawyers of the oil industry—BP, Shell and, in the United States, Aramco, who have developed skills in the laws of the area that are perhaps second to none in the Western world.

There are many difficulties of understanding in this sphere, not the least of which is due to the problems of language; but there are also philosophical differences of approach between lawyers of the Middle East and lawyers of this country and in the United States which need to be identified and explained. My role in interpreting those essential differences reminds me of an Iranian folk story which sums up my situation. A certain Iranian Mullah, or priest, known to many as Mullah Nasrehdeen, was fond of boasting of his wide learning and knowledge of Arabic; when put to the test and asked for the Arabic word for a cow, he was happily able to offer the correct word. But then unfortunately he was asked the Arabic for 'calf'. The good Mullah did not know, but typically did not wish to admit his ignorance. He replied, 'Well, the Arabs are patient people. They wait until the calves grow up and then they call them cows'.

2—The legal system in the Middle East—past and present

The first objective must therefore be to summarise and attempt to explain the wide discrepancy between the legal situation of the Middle East in the past, (when it was dominated almost entirely by the canon law of Islam with its various schools of thought and particular schismatic divisions) with the situation today; in essence the task of explaining the way in which Islamic law has been either displaced or modernised. No consideration will be given therefore to those areas of law where traditional Islamic law has been retained to some degree; i.e. the law of inheritance and family law in general.

The initial problem is the general question of whether there is in fact a Middle East system of law, or whether there are as many systems of law as there are countries in the Middle East. The area is vast and varied and one finds that few people really understand the geography of the area. In fact the writer's father, who was one of the Iranian delegates to the 1945 San Francisco Conference which established the United Nations, happened to be sitting on a committee and was introduced by the Chairman as being the representative of Iran, 'a small flat country situated between the Tigris and Euphrates rivers'. He then got up and said that like the story of the Lord Privy Seal, Iran was neither flat, nor small, nor between the Tigris and the Euphrates. Historically, there has been a truly effective regional centre of power and authority only periodically, and as a result the growth of rival schools of law, rival caliphates and autonomous regions are important factors. The basic factors of unity, have of course been religion, the knowledge of the Arabic language and something of a common economic history. More recently, factors of diversity began to grow as a result of the building of the Suez Canal, followed in turn by the discovery of oil in certain places in the area, and the varied effects of the chequered history of colonialism in its many guises.

Modernisation of the legal system has therefore tended to come at different stages in each country and legal reforms have been stimulated both by the particular political evolution of, and by the pace of economic development in, each of them. So, on a very general basis, the answer is that there are many varied legal systems, but they all share a common origin.

3—The origin and evolution of the system

The starting point of the system is basically the Shari'a. There are several key factors to bear in mind when looking at the Shari'a. First, Islam is not only a religion, it is also a political system. Second, Islamic law, as distinct from Western law, is also very much a system of rules that are enforced, but not created, by the sanction of the state. In Islam the law of God is the law, even if no one enforces it, or even if in certain parts it is unenforceable; the state may, in practice, enforce much that is not consistent with the Islamic law. Third, law was but one facet of the Islamic way or system, but all its elements were intertwined and thus the lawyer was the theologist and the theologist the lawyer.

The Shari'a was much more than law. It was really, and has been so called, 'the whole duty of man'—that is, a code setting out duties, moral theology, spiritual guidance, hygiene, social deportment and courtesy. The Shari'a, in effect, meant a path or a track to be followed to attain salvation.

(a) The basic sources of the Shari'a

Looked at as a legal system, the basic sources of the Shari'a are four:

(i) The Koran—i.e., the Word of God;

(ii) The Sunna—the practice of the Prophet;

(iii) Ijma'a, or the consensus; and

(iv) Qiyas, or analogy.

(i) *The Koran.*—The Koran contains the utterances of the Almighty, communicated in his actual words by the Angel Gabriel to the Prophet. While not a law book or a code, the Koran constitutes an eloquent appeal to mankind, and the Arabs in particular, to obey the law of God as it is already revealed or capable of being discovered. The influence of the Koran on the development of the legal system came about in several ways. The Prophet, as the ruling sovereign, was faced with numerous legal problems on which he sought divine guidance and the answers to these problems constitute a special legal element in the Koran. Some 500 such texts exist of which about 80 are of what could be treated as having a legal nature by Western standards. These texts were then construed by a form of statutory interpretation to extract all possible guidance from them.

The non-legal texts of the Koran, which constituted moral exhortations and divine promises, have also been construed by analogy to afford legal rules. The text: 'Surely they say usury is like sale, but God has made sale lawful and usury unlawful' (Koran 2, 276, 277) provides a good example. Many scholars of Islamic Law feel that this text has had a pervading influence on the whole law of contract, namely that the lawfulness of commercial transactions has to be gauged in terms of their resemblance to sale.

(ii) *The Sunna.*—The Sunna or the practice of the Prophet himself and of his followers constitutes, some feel, a common law of Islam, culled from traditions—i.e., what the Prophet said or did or approved of by his silence. The nature of this source and the unreliability of many of the traditions subsequently collected, led to a feeling of hopelessness in the task of trying to sift the true Sunna from the false.

(iii) *Ijma'a.*—A further source was Ijma'a, or consensus. This was based on the idea that God would not permit his people universally to be in error. This consensus was reckoned to be of two kinds—Ijma, consensus of the whole community, on the one hand, and on the other Ijma, consensus of the Imams or leaders and great teachers.

(iv) *Analogy.*—The other source mentioned was analogy—Qiyas. While authoritative texts of the Koran and the traditions and statements of consensus were commonly referred to as having the highest degree of authority, in contrast, Qiyas was deemed to be rules perceived by reasoning from analogy. This is a less authoritative source of law than the three previous principal sources.

The Shari'a, then, was God's Law and in some ways this dominant characteristic provides the best explanation for the inherent rigidity of the system and for the subsequent failure of the legal system to adapt to change. Islamic lawyers were able to find some initial scope for flexibility by the invention of doctrines justified by the concept of Istihsan—i.e., choosing for the better. In effect, this constitutes a form of equity, but not the Anglo-Saxon idea of equity as a set of legal principles or rules having the effect of setting aside certain over-rigid rules of law. The main use of this concept was to justify setting aside strict Qiyas to abolish or modify an existing or harmful custom, where the application of a strict Qiyas would lead to an unnecessarily harsh result.

(b) Other contributory doctrines

Use was also made, in the early period, of the doctrine of Istislah, an idea of goodwill and reconciliation as an aid to flexibility. The doctrine of Darura, or necessity, was also utilised. This latter doctrine was however used, but sparingly, perhaps because it was repugnant to the inherent fatalism of the pious.

In practice, the main outlines of the Shari'a law were settled during the first three centuries after the Hegira, and no significant innovations occurred thereafter. There were other causes, that contributed to the rigidity of Islamic law, and these should be mentioned in passing. The first of these was a sense that some Western writers have alluded to as 'inherent Arab conservatism'. The other is that Islam never formally recognised the right of any human ruler to do anything but administer the law of God and as a result its lawyers evolved a doctrine of Social Contract, by which the Imam was supposed to have contracted with the people to administer only that law. No real constitutional check ever existed over despotism, however, and only in theory could a breach by the ruler lead to his deposition. As a result, the rigidity and technicality of the Law and the upright character of its expounders, added to the respect that they enjoyed, came to be regarded as constituting the best protection for the common people against abuse by a despot.

This phenomenon, of course, produced a further explanation for the lack of flexibility. It may also be familiar to English Common Law lawyers who may recall that the judges themselves were able to preserve some of the liberty of the subject from the despotism of the Tudors and Stuarts by resorting to the technicalities of the Common Law.

Technicality and formalism thus became major characteristics of the Shari'a, and these were fostered in turn by a rigid and archaic system of procedure and evidence. Unlike other legal systems, alternative means of escape from the rigidity of the system were not available to the Islamic lawyers. There was no concept of equity, in the English sense of the word, little judicial discretion and little possibility of legal fictions. Nor was there much scope for legislation. The human ruler could merely administer the law, The only developments, through Ijma'a and Qiyas, were also eventually institutionalised and, by the end of the third century after the Hegira, jurists were already limited in terms of their ability of going back to original sources and interpreting them.

Gradually, different schools of law were established as jurists tended to draw together on a regional basis in places like Iraq, Medina, Damascus and elsewhere and the faculty of re-examination and interpretation fell into abeyance. Jurists became commentators or produced glosses and then glosses upon glosses and their concentration increasingly focused on the separate schools which formed around the teachings of one or more dominant teachers. In turn these schools were reduced in practice to four: the Hanafi School, the Maliki School, the Shafi'i School, and the Hanbali School.

4—Legal reform in the Middle East

From the end of the third century after the Hegira until the middle of the last century (AD) little change was thus made or indeed felt to be needed. While the Ottoman Empire saw the introduction of some reforms by decree such as Ghanoons and Nizam Nalimehs, always with the thinly veiled illusion of the need to better administer the Shari'a, it was only in the 1850s, with the rise of Western imperialism and the rapid weakening of the power and authority of the Ottoman Empire, that the process of real legal reform in the Middle East began. The Ottoman Sultans began the process of introducing material changes to Islamic Law by legislative means, (although indirectly,) by gradually restricting the competence of the Islamic Shari'a judges or Qadis, while always insisting that their measures were consistent with the Shari'a. This process, begun by the Ottoman Sultans, commenced as early as the reign of Mohammed II, 1451–1481, and was particularly obvious during the reign of Suliman I, 1520–1560. However, the gradual weakening of the Empire and the conflicts with the Shari'a made this a somewhat limited effort, confined to special areas of public law, tax and administration.

The next major development was the effort to prepare legislation on special topics and apply such legislation to both the Moslem and non-Moslem subjects of the Sublime Porte. This became important because of the increasing interference in the internal affairs of the Ottoman Empire by Western governments. The Tanzimat was the major reformist effort of the Ottoman Sultans and commenced with a Code of Commerce in 1850 and thereafter with a whole series of laws based on the models of European, principally French, legislation. These included a Penal Code in 1858, a Code of Commercial Procedure in 1861 and a Code of Maritime Commerce in 1863.

(a) The Majalla in the Ottoman Empire

The effect of this development was to restrict progressively the scope of Shari'a law. Nevertheless the Ottoman Empire did not abandon the Shari'a. Instead, a major effort was made during the period 1869–1876, to codify the Shari'a according to the teachings of the Hanbali School, the school followed essentially by the Ottoman Empire, and to enact it as the law of the Ottoman State.

The product of this effort was the Majalla (its proper title being the Majalla y Ahakemy Adleay) covering, in a series of Articles, the law of contracts and obligations and of civil procedure. This body of law was enacted as the Ottoman Civil Code in 1877. The 'Travaux Préparatoires' explained that the code was required to give clear, authoritative guidance on Islamic law to the newly-created secular courts.

In effect the Majalla is a secular version of Islamic law. The code, however, did contain significant modifications to the Shari'a rules of evidence. The Majalla continued in effect in the former territories of the Ottoman Empire after 1918 where it was applied as the civil law of these new states by their newly established, secular tribunals. This situation prevailed until the enactment of new civil codes in Lebanon in 1932, Syria in 1949 and Iraq in 1953. The law was also applied at times in Cyprus, Israel and Jordan. Interestingly, it never applied to Egypt.

(b) Fatawa al Allam Geviah in India

In India a similar reform effort was to be made by the Moguls, and this was to apply Islamic law on an empire-wide basis, again following the Hanbali doctrine. This effort was known as the Fatawa al Allam Geviah. British rule, however, led to a more restricted application of the Shari'a, i.e., to family and personal law, with an effort being made to allow for the personal law of the Sunnis and Shi'ahs and other sects to be independent of each other. In other areas and in procedure and in evidence, secular law gradually replaced the Shari'a precepts by (i) the introduction of a judiciary trained in English law and equity, (ii) a system of appeals to the Privy Council, and (iii) the application of English precepts such as the doctrine of precedent. By the end of the nineteenth century Islamic law in British India was in essence a special legal system, properly labelled Anglo-Mohammedan law. It is noteworthy that a parallel hybrid development occurred in Palestine where the Majalla was for a period applied in a similar common law setting.

(c) The Code Morand in Algeria

At the same period, in Algeria, at the other extreme of the Islamic world, a somewhat similar phenomenon was being observed. Here the Maliki School had been influential and the French extended the application of the Shari'a as taught by the Maliki School, at the expense of prevailing local customs. An attempt was made in 1916 to enact the Maliki-based code of Algerian Moslem Law incorporating the *Jurisprudence Constante* or Case Law of the local courts and doctrine of French Jurists in Algeria. This code, known as the Code Morand, after Marcel Morand, the French jurist who was active in its preparation, attempted to incorporate numerous doctrines from other Islamic law schools which, in Morand's opinion, were better suited to modern conditions. Though not enacted, the code had great influence and, in essence, Algeria developed what could be termed the special 'Droit Musselman Algérien'. The French made a similar effort in Tunisia to enact codes based on Islamic jurisprudence and applied by secular tribunals. The jurist David Santilana drafted civil and commercial legislation for Tunisia in 1899 incorporating a mixture of Islamic and civil law principles, and this was the basis for the 1906 Tunisian Code of Obligations and Contracts.

(d) Khedive Ismael's Reforms in Egypt

In Egypt, which had attained effective juridical independence from the Ottoman Empire under his rule, Khedive Ismael had embarked (as had Constantinople) on serious legal reforms during the latter half of the nineteenth century. Secular courts were established—mixed courts in 1875 and local courts in 1883. Two civil codes, one for application by the mixed court and the other for application by the domestic (Egyptian) courts, as well as a penal code were enacted.

The civil codes were essentially extensive adaptations of the French codes, and although the civil codes included numerous codified principles of Shari'a law, the Shari'a courts were in effect restricted to matters of personal status and family law.

5—The Western influence

The pattern that thus emerges from what is necessarily a very cursory survey of the legal reforms of the late nineteenth century, is one in which the Shari'a is set gradually on one side in favour of codes derived essentially from the West. In some cases, however, codifications included re-statements of Shari'a law, but procedure and commercial law were, in most cases, borrowed almost entirely from the West and in most cases from France. The question why this was so must now be considered.

As Professor Anderson establishes in his short monograph '*Islamic Law in the Modern World*', it is fairly clear that the reason was not due to any pressure of popular demand for reform—although some came from non-Moslem subjects of the Ottoman Empire—but came from above, from the rulers. Perhaps the major factors were the growing interest in administrative efficiency and national progress, the desire to satisfy foreign opinion and also the fact that conservative opposition to reform was under challenge by progressive nationalist elements who felt the need and the ability to challenge Western critics and remove all justifications for Western interference and special privilege. It may also have developed from the need to free national commerce from the dead hand of the B'ath system and the anti-usury laws.

There may also have been an awareness of the inadequacy of the archaic rules of procedure in evidence and a foreseen need for codes which all educated people could understand. Finally, some people felt that to borrow Western codes and leave the Shari'a intact was preferable to any attempt to modify the Shari'a itself. Their idea was that the Shari'a would always be preserved as 'the Law', as Professor Anderson puts it, 'for a Golden Age'.

6—Capitulations

There was one more, important, factor in the steady trend away from the Shari'a—the need to abolish the system of capitulations. The capitulations must be explained. Although now only of historic interest, they do account for much of the feeling of sensitivity, the regard for sovereignty and the desire to avoid all intrusions on sovereignty which is so prevalent in the law of the Middle East. Basically, the capitulations were part of a system of extra-territorial jurisdiction in favour of foreigners, granted by a pattern of treaties commencing in 1673 with France and perhaps the latest of which was that in 1846 with Russia, that gave citizens of France and Russia, the Netherlands, Austria-Hungary, Sweden, Denmark, Prussia and the United Kingdom the right to have their subjects tried by their own courts—in this case Consular Courts. The capitulations were also regulated by agreement amongst the Big Powers themselves, and this led to the formation of mixed commission systems for deciding disputes between persons who were not nationals of the Ottoman Empire.

The abolition of capitulations in the Ottoman Empire resulted from the nationalist view of them as being restrictions or incursions on their sovereignty as well as from the problems of governing Christian minorities. In effect the government in Constantinople tried to introduce judicial reforms as a method of removing the justification for capitulations. The Tanzimat reform system could also be explained in part on that basis. A series of reforms during the nineteenth century, culminating in 1867 in the right of foreigners to own real estate in the Ottoman Empire, were the foundations of the gradual acceptance by foreigners of the fact that local courts and local law should govern them with respect to those rights. After 1908 and the 'Young Turk' Revolution, Turkey unilaterally abrogated the system of capitulations upon entry into World War I. Although the Armistice and the Treaty of Sèvres saw their re-introduction, the regime of Kamal Attaturk finally abolished the system of capitulations by Article 28 of the Treaty of Lausanne in 1932.

In Egypt the capitulations survived much longer, in effect until 1949. They were better organised in the sense that there was a special, highly skilled system of mixed courts, with judges drawn from different countries, to administer a special code applicable to disputes between foreigners and between Egyptians and foreigners. Two courts, in Alexandria and Cairo, and a Court of Appeals in Cairo administered this system, and, as a result, the system survived much longer than in Turkey. However, in 1937 by the Treaty of Montreux it was generally agreed that the capitulations would be abolished by 1949 and the Egyptians set about establishing a system of courts and a new Civil Code (one single civil code applicable to all) which was introduced in 1949 at the same time that the capitulations were finally abolished.

The capitulations are important because they began as a logical extension of the idea of a personal law for non-believing foreigners, i.e., the Moslem law applied only to Moslems, but they inevitably became a focus for nationalism. They encouraged the pattern of secularisation and modernisation of the local law and they led to the receptivity of the local lawyers and the political community to the practice of borrowing foreign law. This may explain the major influence of Western law in the countries in which capitulations existed.

7—Recent influences

By 1915 the commercial and penal laws of the Near East (always of greatest interest to foreigners) had been essentially westernised, both in substance and in terms of the courts applying them. The laws of contract and tort were being applied by secular courts, even though here the substantative law was organised in codes which, though Western in form, were essentially Shari'a-based in substance. Only family law in the widest sense was being still applied by the old fashioned courts from old rules and books in the traditional manner by the traditional officers. Since 1915, the major effort has been to remove the last major vestiges of the old system in all but name.

(i) *Turkey.*—In Turkey the end of the Ottoman Empire saw the enactment of numerous reformist measures; not the least was the decision to discontinue efforts not only to revise the Majalla but to modernise it by incorporating principles of foreign law. Kamal Attaturk decided in 1926 to cast aside this effort completely and simply adopted the Swiss Civil Code and Code of Obligations.

(ii) *Egypt and the influence of Egyptian reforms.*—Returning to the Arab world, the pattern there is one of parallel effort, starting somewhat later than in the rest of the Ottoman Empire. The Egyptian Revolution of Nasser produced a number of reforms: in 1952 private and family Waqfs were abolished and the liquidation of existing Waqfs was ordered. In 1956 the Shari'a courts were abolished and a system of regular courts was introduced in their place. The preparation of a comprehensive code of personal and family law was begun. In 1948 the Egyptian civil code was enacted. This is a very important code because it was drafted largely under the aegis of Professor Sanhouri, a most distinguished Egyptian lawyer. It was based not only on the two earlier civil codes mentioned but also on a codification of the case law of the Egyptian courts, which had been faithfully recorded and well presented. Comparative law as well as recourse to relevant principles of Islamic law were also important in the drafting of this code. The result was to establish a truly national law based on Egypt's old cultural heritage.

Article 1 of the Egyptian Civil Code will be of interest to Common Law lawyers. It states that in default of any relevant provision in the code, i.e., *lacunae*, the court is to be guided by customary law, principles of Islamic law and natural justice. When accused of having done away with the last vestiges of the Shari'a, Professor Sanhouri replied: 'I assure you that we did not leave a single sound proposal of the Shari'a that we could have included in this legislation without so doing'.

The Egyptian reforms have been instrumental in prompting or encouraging recent changes in legislation by other countries in the area. In 1951 the Jordanians introduced a revised law of family rights to replace the old Ottoman code. Syria, in 1949, replaced the Majalla with a civil code, essentially the Egyptian code with special sections on proof and real property. In 1949 they also abolished private and family Waqfs and in 1953 they introduced a revised law of personal status. Tunisia also saw, in 1957, a revision in the law of personal status as did Morocco in 1958.

Lebanon, in 1932, as mentioned, had adopted a code covering obligations and contracts based on the French model, whereas Libya adopted essentially the Egyptian civil code. Iraq prepared a new civil code in 1951. Again, Professor Sanhouri was very influential, However, in this case there was a far greater effort to incorporate provisions of Islamic law and much was borrowed from the Majalla. The conscious aim was to Arabise, and thereby limit, the French influence. In the last few years Kuwait, Bahrain, the United Arab Emirates and Qatar have taken strong steps to modernise their legal systems, and again the influences of the Egyptian and the Iraqi models of civil codes have been extremely influential. Egyptian lawyers and Palestinian lawyers, schooled in the modernisation of the laws of those countries, have been very active in helping in this process.

(iii) *Saudi Arabia and Oman.*—There remain two major areas, the Sheikdoms in the Gulf and Saudi Arabia, where the Shari'a still applies. Oman and Saudi Arabia are two that can be quoted as examples, although even in these territories the introduction of major amendments to the law has been made, though on a piecemeal basis. In Saudi Arabia this has occurred through the use of 'regulations' rather than 'laws'. For example, in Saudi Arabia the 1850 Ottoman Commercial Code was made applicable. In Oman a new banking law has been drafted and promulgated which is based essentially, and with some novelty, on the Uniform Commercial Code of the United States.

(iv) *Iran.*—In Iran, as in the rest of the Muslim world, the Shari'a courts were weak. There was a great deal of confusion, and no apparent consistency in application of the law. While before 1900 a supreme court or Divon Honay Ahrdla existed, it had no law to apply, no code and no real set of rules and was hence very inactive. Early reforms in Iran came with the adoption of a constitution after the revolution at the turn of the century. This was in the form of a Fundamental Law in 1906 and a supplement to it of 1907. Interestingly enough, this law has a close parallel in the Belgian constitution and the reason for this is quite simple. At the time of the revolution, the revolutionaries locked themselves up in the British Embassy and refused to come out until the constitution was granted. After a great deal of pressure the Qajar Shah then agreed to grant the constitution and sent a message to the Embassy, which was surrounded, to say that if they produced a constitution he would consider it favourably. They rummaged around the Embassy to look for a constitution and reportedly the Ambassador, having come from a previous post in Brussels, happened to have a copy of the Belgian constitution in his possession!

1907 saw the creation of four skeleton non-Shari'a courts—a court of property and financial claims (sometimes known as the court of pecuniary and property claims), a criminal court, a court of appeal and a Divon Honay, or supreme court of appeal. These courts, in effect, had a very nominal role. No codes existed and the courts were supposed to follow the Shari'a both in substance and procedure. Foreign capitulations also existed in Iran. The result of this situation was to lead to disputes on judgements and to appeals from these courts to the Mujtaheeds, who gave conflicting opinions and invariably disagreed with the civil courts.

In 1908, in an effort to solve this problem, a Court of Conflicts was created to provide a measure of uniformity between these different tribunals. It was still difficult, though, to persuade the clergy to agree to any reform.

1910 saw the creation of the office of an Attorney General and in

1911 the Ministry of Justice was reformed. A Judiciary Committee of the Majlis or Parliament was established to consider new experimental codes and a committee of experts was formed under the chairmanship of an influential French jurist, Adolphe Pierny, who was chargėd with drafting a civil code. This civil code, together with the other codes that were in preparation was always worked on the basis and justified as being, of an experimental nature. This was stressed to circumvent the opposition of the clergy, who, of course, relied on the Islamic guarantee contained in Article 2 of the supplement to the Fundamental Law in the Constitution of 1907, which provided that no laws could be enacted contrary to the Shari'a. In 1915, again on this 'experimental' basis, a temporary commercial code was introduced. Difficulties existed for the new courts—there was a shortage of staff who were unfamiliar with the principles they were supposed to apply, and as a result there was a gradual return to the Shari'a courts and to arbitration. Meanwhile the capitulary regime continued for foreigners.

The next major development was the 'second revolution' and with it the accession to power of Reza Shah the Great, first as Prime Minister and then as Sovereign. When Prime Minister he pledged himself to reform the judicial system, his main aims being (as with earlier reforms in Turkey and in Egypt) to abolish the capitulations and to assert nationalist objectives through a reform of legislation. In 1924 an experimental commercial and penal code was prepared and this was introduced in 1926. In 1927 the Ministry of Justice was dissolved and new, foreign, French-trained officials were brought in to take over the administration of justice. In a speech of 1927 Reza Shah stressed: 'The prestige of a nation depends upon the quality of its justice, and I expect of you the most honourable conduct that will at once bring justice and prestige to our country'. This nationalist effort was led by the gifted Minister of Justice, known as Davar, who had studied law extensively in Europe.

In 1928 a Commission, chaired by Minister of Justice Davar, began work on the preparation of a secular civil code and in due course adopted the first volume which went to the Majlis or Parliament and again was justified for enactment on the basis that it was experimental. Also presented to Parliament was a judicial re-organisation bill setting up a hierarchy of courts. The Civil Code of Iran was in part a secularisation of the Shi'ah sect of Islam's version of the Shari'a and was in part based on the French, Belgian and Swiss models. The organization of the code followed to a large extent that of the

French Code Civil. The first ten articles of the Civil Code of Iran, interestingly enough, are almost a direct copy of this. The personal status provisions constituted a codification and simplification or unification of the Shari'a principles. The introduction of this new Civil Code was used as a justification at the same time for the abolition of capitulations.

Thereafter there followed a series of bills throughout 1928, 1929 and 1930. Again, the laws were all being passed for trial periods, the theory being that shortcomings could be corrected before the bills were submitted for permanent enactment. Between 1928–1930 laws appeared regulating trust funds, damages, proof, claims against the state, *cautio judicatum solvi* (trial costs of aliens), the limits of jurisdiction of the Shari'a courts, the use of court injunctions and the law of inheritance. Some of these laws proved impracticable and had to be repealed. In 1929 two final sections of the Civil Code were prepared and the Majlis rejected them twice. In 1935 the final two sections of the Civil Code were adopted.

In the following year Reza Shah again declared that the reforms should now become permanent and on 17th March, 1932, a very heavy blow was struck at the clergy through the introduction of a new law on the registration of documents and property. This, in effect, created a civil register and did away with a major source of income of the clergy. In 1936 the process of secularisation was effectively completed by the enactment of a law on the re-organisation of the judicial system. During the period 1937 to 1939 further laws were enacted on the practice of law and on the use of legal experts. A law of bankruptcy was enacted in 1939. The Code of Civil Procedure which had undergone revision, was introduced in its final version during 1939-40.

The structure of the courts and jurisdiction and the role of the officers of the courts during this period were all subject to reform and here, as in the drafting of the main substantive laws, the influence of the French was extremely striking. This influence could also be detected in the laws relating to the practice and procedure of expropriation as well as in the general law of civil procedure. This influence is not hard to explain. In the decade 1929–39 a long succession of French and Italian law professors arrived in Tehran and began the process of teaching a new class of Iranian-trained lawyers. French advisers sat in the Ministry of Justice. It should also be noted that in 1926 a tentative penal code was adopted, based on German and Italian models which finally became law in 1940.

It would also be timely to list briefly some of the more recent legislation, occurring since the last war. This has been less French in orientation, being based essentially on drafts prepared in Iran by Iranians, with other influences coming into play. One of the major statutes is the Law for the Attraction and Protection of Foreign Investments, adopted in 1955. In 1960 a Law of Civil Responsibility was enacted to take account of the fact that the sections on civil responsibility, or torts, in the civil law had been essentially Shari'a-based and had proved to be unworkable in the light of modern developments. The 1960 Law of Civil Responsibility of Iran is, in effect, an adaptation of the French law based on the relevant sections of the French civil code and a codification of the case law of the French Courts on those articles. In 1967 a revised income tax law was introduced. This law, by the way, is again under revision. In 1967 family law was modernised and in 1969 a new, completely revised law on Joint Stock Companies was introduced. During this period since the Second World War, extensive legislation has also been enacted relating to land ownership, land reform, emancipation of women, profit sharing in industry and the break-up of state monopolies. Houses of equity and arbitration councils have been established to provide speedy justice at first instance and, finally, an Iranian Maritime Code has been introduced.

8—Administrative law problems

It is also desirable to consider certain problems of administrative law, i.e., the relationship between the state and the subject, because that also affects foreign businessmen in the Middle East. Given the influence of the French, their concept of administrative law as a separate body of law regulating the relationship between the state and its citizens had some bearing on the way lawyers in the area analysed these problems. Steps were taken in Turkey to establish a Council of State and a separate system of administrative courts and law along the lines of the French Conseil D'Etat and Droit Administratif. A similar Council of State was established in Lebanon and also in Egypt. Iran always had the concept of a Council of State under consideration, but this was never introduced for political reasons. It was felt by many in the Lower House of Parliament (Majless) that such a Council of State, because of its traditional legislative functions in France, might have an inhibiting effect on the role of Parliament.

Nevertheless, in the Middle East the system of administrative law in embryo exists along the French pattern, but the problem is that there has been really no effort to develop it and there is no body of case law such as there is in France to help to guide these courts. Possibly as a result of this, a lack of confidence has been expressed by foreign businessmen and investors in the ability of the local courts to provide a workable system of justice in terms of settling disputes between foreign companies and governments. The result of this suspicion has been the prevailing use of arbitration clauses. A good example of the use of arbitration is provided by the famous arbitration between Saudi Arabia and Aramco. The arbitrators' report award in this case runs to hundreds of pages and constitutes a not entirely successful but nevertheless fascinating attempt to set up a separate system of law to be applied by the arbitrators, based on the concept of the contract as the law of the parties.

The same conscious feeling of the need for assertions of sovereignty, coupled with the feeling of resentment against the capitulations pervades this whole area of law and, as a result, the governments of these countries are extremely reluctant to agree to arbitration. This feeling has been fortified, understandably in some cases, by the vestiges of the French doctrine which forbids the French Government, or any of its state organs, to agree to arbitration for what are classified as internal contracts. (French case law, it should be noted, does accept the fact that the French Government, or French state agencies, can agree to arbitration for what they classify as international contracts.) As a result of this highly political background, this is a somewhat specialised field of law. There are numerous special statutes on the books and a great deal of caution must be demonstrated by foreign businessmen in attempting to arrive at what may seem to them to be the optimum system for handling of disputes arising from major supply contracts, civil works contracts or as a result of direct investments in industry.

In many respects this situation reflects a major shortcoming of the reforms in the Middle East and it is one sphere in which many observers feel that it is incumbent on the governments of the area not only to develop a system of administrative courts and administrative law in which foreigners can have no excuse for lack of confidence, but also to remove the last vestiges of the old system, and thereby irrefutably justify the use of local courts for all such cases. Regrettably little progress seems to have been made at the present time perhaps because such legislation enjoys only low priority in an area of the World which is today so much on the move.

9—Conclusion

The main feature of the legal history of the Middle East and of the modernisation of its law has therefore, been the decreasing relevance of the Shari'a law. However, it is still clearly important to have an understanding of the background, not only because the language of the law, being essentially Arabic, is based on Arabic concepts (i.e., the Shari'a concepts), but also because certain areas of the law and the modern codes in places such as Iran, Iraq, Egypt, Syria, still retain elements of Shari'a law embodied in them. To understand these codes properly the background of the law of contract and obligations has to be comprehended and the Shari'a must be referred to. Obviously, for a country such as Saudi Arabia and for certain areas in the Gulf, the Shari'a law is still the basic law, with a few fields, such as tax, the law of commerce, *inter alia*, where specific legislation has been introduced.

One other significant problem which should be mentioned in this connection is the question of how to find the relevant law. The author has had, in the last few years, a number of occasions to appear as an expert witness on foreign law. One of the difficulties in the Common Law world of pleading and proving foreign law is the Common Law judges' natural desire for precedents and, therefore, for a view of the case law of the countries. In a country like Iran, apart from a rather feeble effort during the late 1930s to collect the judgements of the newly established secular courts, there has been until the very recent past no record to speak of of the judgements of the Iranian courts. Indeed the major effort that has been made to date has been the result of the private endeavours of one of the distinguished practising lawyers at the Bar who persuaded a local newspaper first to produce a compilation of the legislation in force and second, to make a compilation of case law. In this respect Iran is probably further behind than Egypt and the other Arab countries of the Levant, where the model of the French was followed more closely and much earlier and where it is easier to find the sources of law. But in a country like Iran it is still extremely difficult. In sum therefore there is no substitute for the use of the local lawyer and his experience. It is clearly too facile to think that the codes as printed in English furnish any meaningful understanding of the legal system or of the laws themselves.

Questions and Answers

Question

Our firm has dealt with Arab governments for 50 years. They do breach their contracts. Is there an Islamic religious excuse for this?

Answer

The Saudi Arabia/Aramco arbitral award should be studied in relation to this question. In effect, the arbitration agreement between Aramco (the Arabian American Oil Company) and Saudi Arabia contained stipulations that both parties regarded contracts as binding. It would also be of interest to look at the writings of the distinguished jurist Ibn Taymia, who deals at some length with the concept of contract.

One of the interesting arguments in the Arabian American Oil Company arbitration was that in which counsel for the Government attempted to establish that there was a concept in the law of Saudi Arabia permitting the revision of government contracts in the light of changed circumstances, rather along the lines of the French administrative doctrine of 'contrat administratif' which gives the state the power to amend contracts in the public interest with detailed rules on how to calculate compensation. In contrast, Aramco, which had been encouraged by the late King Ibn Saud to send its lawyers to the Middle East to study the Shari'a, came up with arguments based on the writings of the scholar Ibn Taymia to the effect that under Islamic law there is no distinction in contract between public contracts—i.e., administrative or government contracts—and private contracts. In all contracts there was equality of the contracting parties and both parties were bound to their promise in the same manner as each other regardless of whether one was a state and the other was a private individual. The arbitration award in effect came down in favour of the Arabian American Oil Company. (The key issue related to the government's wish to direct the company to use tankers owned by Onassis which Aramco alleged would be in conflict with the provisions of the concession.) The award, it should be noted, relied heavily for its interpretation of the contract on general principles of law and on the usages and customs of the oil industry.

My own personal feeling about that arbitration award is that a proper application of the Shari'a and its concise and clear concepts of contractual interpretation should have led to an award in favour of Saudi Arabia and this may explain why there has been an increasing reluctance on the part of the Saudi Arabians to submit disputes to international arbitration again. But nevertheless, there is a considerable body of Islamic law on the subject of the binding nature of contracts and in particular the relationship between the government as a contracting party and a private individual.

Question

It has been said that there is no substitute for using a local lawyer. How is the profession organised in the Middle East?

Answer

The organisation of the profession in the Middle East, in particular in the countries of North Africa, Egypt, Lebanon, as well as in Turkey and Iran, is along the lines of the Bar as organised in France. The system of recruitment of judges and their appointment as officials in the Ministry of Justice, the organisation of the Bar and the rules on the relative roles of the notary and the attorney are very similar in practice to those of France. The Bar, however, is a much newer institution and the rules such as discipline have been applied for far fewer years. This simple comparison therefore leaves a lot to be desired. But nevertheless the system is basically that adapted from the French.

Question

Is there anything like the bâtonnier system which they have in France for the local leader of the Bar?

Answer

There is a very similar system. A senior representative of the Bar is the leader of the Bar Association.

Question

What are the basic differences between Iran and the countries of the Arabian Peninsula?

Answer

Iran is not an Arab country. Persian, not Arabic, is the national tongue. One of the features of the difference between Iran and the Arab countries is, of course, religion. Iran follows the Shi'ah school of Islam, whereas the Arabs and the Turks, and to the greatest extent the Pakistanis and other parts of the Arab world, are Sunni. The difference—and this is at best a gross over-simplification—is roughly the same as the distinction between the Catholic and the Protestant schools of Christianity. It was used at the height of the Ottoman Empire by the Iranian sovereigns, particularly Shah Abbas the Great, to bring unity to what is now Iran and to produce a cohesive force which enabled them to resist the incursions by the Ottomans. The other Arab countries were not able to do this. So nationalism in Iran was fostered on the basis of a religious and linguistic, rather than racial, distinction.

Practical, Financial and Legal Considerations for Companies doing Business in Arab Countries

by

Dr Jamal Nasir,
B.A., Ph.D. (Lond.), Barrister

Dr. Nasir is a Member of the Jordan Bar and other Arab Bar Counsel on all questions of Arab Law, a Barrister of the Federal Supreme Court of Nigeria, and a former Minister of Justice of Jordan.

1—The scope for, and attitudes to, business in Arab countries

The area under consideration is now one of major importance, as far as business is concerned. There is a demand for industry, construction, agriculture, transport and consumer goods. The Arab countries today possess all the elements needed for the expansion of business in all these fields. There is the large population (over 100,000,000); there are the resources and the necessary funds; and there is the development, and the need for development, in every field.

There is one other factor which is very important and that is the determination and the will of those in power, as well as the people of the countries concerned, to develop their countries and to use the resources of the world to bring about modern development and with it, the introduction of the latest technology. This is a very important factor in that it has really given an additional incentive to education in the Middle East. Jordan alone has something like over 40,000 students scattered all over the world; thousands of others, from different Arab countries, are also studying abroad. They specialise in engineering, medicine, economics and various other subjects. The training which these students receive forms a sound basis for a thorough appreciation and application of modern technology and development in the Middle East.

The Arab world of today stands, as it has always done, between East and West. But having the resources and the finance, as they do at present, gives the Arab countries an added incentive to maintain their own development in line with that which is going on in different parts of the world. Until recently, the area had been dismissed as being of only secondary importance, but now its significance is becoming more and more apparent to all. This importance of the Arab world was mainly realised after the energy crisis in 1973 which showed beyond all doubt that although this was an area in need of development, it was nevertheless capable of understanding and applying modern methods of technology.

Business men who go out to the Arab countries must, from the outset, understand that when they arrive in the Middle East they are going to be dealing with people who are more or less their equals. So they should not try to be, nor should they give the impression of being, superior to their Arab counterparts in knowledge and expertise. Many people realise from their own experience that Arab businessmen are shrewd, know exactly what they want and precisely how much they would like to get out of the party who is going to do business with them!

Before a businessman enters into an agreement he should be absolutely certain in his mind that he is able to fulfil his obligations under it. This is most important because over and over again experience has shown that when a businessman enters into an agreement casually and then suddenly either neglects the agreement or simply does not fulfil his obligations under it, this results in complications, financial loss and misunderstanding leading to litigation.

While sympathising with the problems and difficulties caused by strikes in England, the Arab businessman expects that once a contract has been entered into under which goods are promised, any delay must be kept to the absolute minimum. Certainly no delay should occur in producing bonds and guarantees for the commencement of the work. There have been cases where contracts have been signed but the bonds and the guarantees necessary were held up, and the contract had to be cancelled as a result.

2—The practical aspect

(a) Government projects

Government projects can be in various fields, and are mainly concerned with construction of industry, agriculture and transport.

These projects can either be entered into with the government as the result of open tender or as the result of direct negotiation. The Arab government concerned might consider that a certain project is so important to the national interest that it will decide to negotiate that contract with a selected group of those companies which it considers are the most qualified to do the job. In such a case the government concerned will require the company or the manufacturer chosen to enter into some form of partnership with them—in other words, to take part in the equity. This arises not so much from the financial help that the company can give, but should be seen more as a demonstration of goodwill and as an indication that the company really is able to fulfil its obligations. In many cases, of course, the companies chosen contribute their share through the form of technical assistance and knowledge, whilst the financial aspect is covered by the government concerned.

But where a project is to be undertaken by tender, then it will be a question of international tender, normally open to many countries and all sorts of companies are invited. Every aspect of the project is well defined and adequate details are given in the invitation to tender.

In almost all cases, the law of the country concerned would require that any contract with a foreign company should be regulated and governed by local law. This is a question of prestige, and the Arab government would normally insist on having its national law apply. Some States insist that, in the event of a dispute, this should be referred to the local court; others incorporate an arbitration clause. This course is becoming more and more frequent. The question of arbitration can be settled by providing for arbitration either locally or by the International Chamber of Commerce in Paris. The idea of arbitration is attractive both to the foreign company and to the government or the individual concerned, as it saves time by proceeding quickly and privately and brings a speedy end to a dispute instead of allowing it to linger on in court.

(b) Private sector contracts

Contracts in this sector can be either with private companies or with individuals and they may take the form of a joint venture, involving local interest and participation. In such cases again, it is the general principle that local laws will apply.

There are, nevertheless, many contracts where a clause is inserted providing that in the event of a dispute, English law should apply and that arbitration should take place in England. This has gradually been accepted and this trend is becoming more apparent. When discussing the type of arbitration and the type of law to govern the contract, it is often easier to reach agreement with an individual or company than with a government which, as already mentioned, normally insists that local law should govern the contract. Some factors to be considered when making contracts in the private section are as follows:

(i) *Disadvantages of contracting with individuals.*—Whenever possible, if a company wishes to enter into an agreement in the private, non-government sector, it is better to do so with another company rather than with an individual. The reason for this is that if the particular individual dies, the question of inheritance becomes a complicated matter depending on the rules of the Muslim law of inheritance, which are complex.

(ii) *Translation of contracts.*—Another important factor is the question of translation. Once an agreement has been entered into there should be a corresponding Arabic text attached to the English text. This Arabic text or translation must be agreed from the very beginning.

There are two reasons for providing a translation. The first is that because Arabic is a very rich language, it is possible to translate different agreements by giving each a different interpretation. Grammatically, the Arabic text is correct on each occasion, but once an English text has been agreed, then it must be ensured that the Arabic translation is the correct translation both of the spirit and of the letter of the agreement. This Arabic translation can be attached to the contract in English, which should also contain a provision to the effect that the attached translation is agreed.

The second reason is that, in carrying out the terms of the contract reference will have to be made to the contract itself, particularly when dealing with Arab nationals in Government departments or business. If their help is sought over one of the terms of the contract, then, obviously, they will benefit from having sight of a correct Arabic translation.

(iii) *Training of personnel.*—The question of training personnel is most important in the Middle East. It is vitally important that any foreign businessman or company wishing to undertake some project in the Middle East or to take part in a tender should specify clearly that facilities will be provided to train the personnel of the country concerned. This is very attractive and acceptable to those countries, because they are keen for their nationals to be trained so that eventually they may take over the direct management of the project.

In the case of a tender, preference is often given to a company which has indicated a willingness to train such personnel.

(iv) *Insurance.*—Another factor is the question of insurance. Once an agreement has been entered into, care should be taken to see that insurance is adequate. This is particularly so when local personnel are employed—they should be well covered either by the company or by the joint venture in which that company is taking part. Somebody must be responsible for compensation in the event of injury or death. Many Arab countries have local Insurance Companies.

(c) Supply of goods or machinery
The supply of goods or machinery is a straightforward type of transaction but the supplier, to avoid complications, should endeavour to fulfil the exact terms of the contract, paying particular attention to such matters as delivery dates and quantity and quality of goods.

When machinery is supplied manufacturers should provide adequate spares, because if the machinery goes wrong, blame will fall not on the spare parts that are missing, or which have been inadequately purchased, but on the machine and its manufacturer. The manufacturer, to protect his reputation, should insist that adequate spares are purchased and delivered.

3—Representation of companies in the Middle East

The question of commercial representation is an important aspect of business in the Middle East and there are three principal ways in which this can be achieved.

(a) By representative
It is a foregone conclusion that a great deal will depend upon the representative or commercial representative that a company has in the various Arab countries concerned. A company that has interests in the Arab world should be absolutely certain to choose an able and responsible person who is well informed and capable of negotiating. It cannot be overstated that a badly represented company suffers a great deal.

There should also be a certain amount of co-ordination and co-operation between the commercial representatives of different firms. In spite of the normal competition that exists between them, if, say, five or six British companies dealing in the same line send their representatives to the Middle East, it is not really in their best interests that each one should start competing with the other. It is better that they should work out among themselves some sort of a co-ordinating formula which would enable them to put across the good aspects of each company and at the same time avoid prejudicial criticism of themselves and their competitors.

When negotiations take place with Arab companies or with Arab governments it is advisable that whoever is responsible for the conduct of the affairs of the company should select as negotiators senior representatives of his company to match the seniority and the status of the person on the other side.

Finally, the commercial representative of a company in the Middle East should always bear in mind that his function is to do the job his company has sent him to do and he should avoid at all times the temptation to meddle or take an active interest in political discussion.

(b) By publicity and literature
The company concerned should also prepare its literature well and, wherever possible, give complete information about itself and about the jobs it has done in the past. It would help also if it could give bank references, because such information gives an idea of the status and the position of the company. Furthermore, each company, once it has taken on a job, or even when it is in the process of taking it on, should have some sort of a liaison man, a local person who is able to follow up matters in the various government departments and have dealings with the locals. He would probably prove to be more satisfactory than, say, an expatriate representative. This is important and can be most beneficial for the company concerned.

(c) By agents
A third way in which a company can be commercially represented is by giving its agency to someone based in the Middle East. A company which adopts this method should be very careful to select the right type of agent. He must be chosen with great care because, once an agent has been appointed, he cannot be easily dismissed. This somewhat inflexible stand was first taken in the Lebanon and the trend now is being followed in the other Arab countries. The agent acquires certain rights from the law, rather than from the terms of the agency that he holds from the company. The law in Lebanon, for instance, protects him and gives him privileges that the principal can do nothing about. Experience has shown that a number of leading firms in Great Britain who have attempted to change their agents, have found the amount of claims against them so substantial that they have been obliged, for the present at least, to maintain the status quo. There are various ways and means of getting around these restrictions, but as a cautionary principle, agents should be very carefully chosen.

4—The financial aspect

Finally, consideration must be given to the financial aspect. It must not be assumed that just because the Arab countries of today are enjoying a healthy balance of payments that there is surplus liquidity and that the Arab businessman will easily part with his money. The Arabs are shrewd, they understand what they have, they understand what they want, and they are becoming very experienced in their investments and in deciding how best to use their money. Raising money in the Arab countries can be done in a variety of ways and much will depend on the standing of the borrowing company and its ability to raise money in the banks locally. The standing of the businessman himself is also an important factor and is frequently instrumental in encouraging the raising of money comparatively quickly.

The tendency at present is to expect the direct financial or technical participation of foreign companies, rather than a straightforward contract of sale. The Arab government in question would usually prefer the contracting foreign company, as a demonstration of its belief and commitment to the contract, to guarantee that it will be implemented and the project satisfactorily completed. On the question of participation a foreign company is better placed if it offers as much as it can on the technical aspect, or on the know-how, rather than on the financial aspect.

The banking procedure in the area is broadly similar to the banking procedures that exist in every European country and in America—there are British, European, American banks as well as many Arab banks which enjoy a first class reputation.

The facilities are subject to local regulations, but are generally in line with the practice in Western countries. In some countries the local regulations are very acceptable. Lebanon, as well as many other Arab countries, permits the unrestricted transfer of money. It is not a very complicated procedure to satisfy the necessary local regulations and to have permits granted. Bank guarantees from first class banks are very much used in Saudi Arabia, Kuwait, the Arab Emirates, the Lebanon, Egypt and Jordan, for example. Against such bank guarantees a company can easily raise loans from a local bank.

5—Formation of companies: a brief summary

The requirements for the formation of companies in Arab countries are fundamentally similar to the requirements of the Companies Acts of 1948 and 1967 in the United Kingdom. There are differences of course, so each case has to be looked at on its own. It should be noted that a certain proportion of the shares will have to be issued to the nationals of the country concerned and the Head Office of the Company will have to be in that country. Besides companies limited by shares, there are unlimited companies as well as partnerships. The contents of the formation document should give the name of the company and its objects, and stipulate the limitation of the liability of the members and the amount of the share capital.

It is possible, in most of the Arab countries, for foreign companies to open a branch or have a representative. This would need to be registered and for registration the Memorandum and Articles of Association and particulars about the various directors should be submitted.

Some Arab countries make it a pre-requisite that the country of origin of the company concerned will give the same facilities to Arab companies from the country concerned. This presents no problem because on the whole there is no restriction in Europe on foreign-owned companies.

6—Insurance

The question of insurance is an important one. Some companies insist that the shippers should obtain insurance. Certain countries, Jordan for instance, require a local insurance company to insure the goods. But the insurance principles are the same as those in the United Kingdom. Once a company has business in a Middle East country it should thereafter insure with one of the best local insurance companies.

Questions and Answers

Question

Is the limited right of termination the same for distributors as well as agents? Does it matter that the distributor agreement is subject to English law, where no compensation is payable?

Answer

It should be made quite clear in the English text of the contract that the distributor has no agency rights and has only a limited amount of authority conferred on him. A company should always emphasise that the distributor merely purchases goods from the company, distributing them himself. He has no obligation to the company as its agent, and is not representing and speaking on its behalf.

Question

Is there a government department in the United Arab Emirates as such to deal with contracts, or does each Sheikh deal personally with specific contracts?

Answer

There is a department that deals with contracts. In fact it is run by one of the most brilliant Sheikhs of that area—a man called Sheikh Hamdan. His department has many engineers mainly from Jordan, Egypt, Pakistan and Iran. These engineers are really quite capable of dealing with the problems that arise, so the States are more and more inclined to centralise this activity.

Question

Are most agreements in the Lebanon in French or in Arabic? Should an Arabic translation be attached to English agreements, or perhaps a French translation? Furthermore, where there are agreed English and Arabic texts of a contract, but the Arab government party to the contract requires that the contract contains a provision that both texts control the interpretation of the contract, or else that the Arab text governs, how much would a local court deal with a problem of interpretation under the contract?

Answer

In Lebanon agreements are in Arabic. There is no question of using French. It is not the official language, so Arabic must be the text that will be relied upon in case of any dispute in court and so forth. And besides, in implementing the contract, it would be necessary to refer directly to the Arabic text.

As to the rest of the question, the Arabic text is the one that will govern the contract. The court will look at the Arabic text and rely on it as the text that governs the relationship of the parties.

Question

If a United Kingdom company were to establish a subsidiary in, say, Syria, with local participation, would there be any impediments to its operating in countries other than the Middle East?

Answer

No, there would be no difficulty, but it should comply with certain formalities of registration. In Syria the company must operate in one of the three free zones to have a subsidiary with local participation.

If a company is registered in the Lebanon, and it operates a contract in the Lebanon and wants to go to Jordan and register and carry out a contract in Jordan (which happens very often) then it would be in the interests of the company concerned, and indeed a requirement by the Jordan government, that the company should also register in Jordan.

Question

Are there any restrictions on the ownership of land (*a*) by an English company or (*b*) by a local company with a majority stake held by an English company, in Saudi Arabia and Oman in particular?

Answer

I think you can take it that restriction on holding land is a general rule throughout the Arab world. So a foreign company must not think of acquiring any interest as such either as a foreign investment or as a foreign land holding company, because this is bound to complicate matters for it. Usually those countries concerned are very jealous of the idea that foreigners are owning land in that particular country.

Question

Is it a general requirement of Arab countries that negotiating personnel require powers of attorney, so that the final contract can be actually signed in the country itself?

Answer

This is a very important requirement. When a company sends somebody to talk to or enter into any form of agreement with any country on behalf of a foreign company, this representative should have a full power of attorney drawn, say, by a solicitor in this country, or signed before a notary public, or commissioner of oaths. It must also be certified and must be signed before a notary public, who will then take it to have it certified and signed by the Foreign Office and by the embassy of the country concerned. Without having it certified by the embassy of the country concerned it will have no legal binding effect of any kind and will not be accepted.

Question

What is the legal position if a contract with a government or ruler includes a provision that is contrary to local law, e.g. international arbitration or the payment of interest?

Answer

First of all, such a contract would not normally be passed by the various government departments in the country concerned, as it is going to be contrary to the provision of local law. It may be that there are certain rulers in some areas who enter into an agreement that does not take into consideration the local law because it has not been established or it has not been developed as completely as it should be, but this is being eliminated. It would be advisable, and in the interest of the party negotiating the contract, to see that the contract is binding and legal not only as signed by the person concerned, but also according to the local laws.

Question

Is it true that the best way to protect the interests of the foreign party is to insert in the agreement (1) an arbitration clause providing for arbitration abroad, for example the International Chamber of Commerce, and (2) a clause to the effect that the controlling text in any controversy is the one written in the foreign language?

Answer

As a general principle it should be understood that terms cannot be dictated to the other side. If a company wishes certain terms regarding arbitration, then it is up to that company to demonstrate that it is in the interests of both parties to do so, having regard to convenience, speed and so on.

Secondly, the foreign text of the agreement cannot be made to be accepted as being binding because that is not practical (even if it was accepted by an individual or by a government). It is very unlikely that a government would accept that a foreign text would be binding as, in the event of a dispute, it goes to their court and that court will have to have a translation anyway.

Tax Considerations

by

Julian F. K. Lee

Julian Lee is a Chartered Accountant who has specialised in international taxation for a number of years. He is a tax partner in the London office of a firm of chartered accountants and supervises their international tax practice in London.

1—General considerations

As with any other area of taxation, when a company considers the question of doing business in the Middle East, it has to decide whether it is doing business 'in' or 'with', and it must examine three separate areas relating to the activity:

(1) in terms of the home country's tax and accounting aspects, the company must first look at the required, desired or likely post-tax return in that home country;

(2) it should also consider existing international tax planning in other locations (including any regulatory requirements in the home or other countries); and

(3) it must look at the local tax planning possibilities in the country of investment.

Taking the analysis of the home environment as read, a company should then consider its existing international position. Its operations may have been structured through a domestic or foreign holding company, or it may have existing loss carry-overs in certain countries that have been difficult to utilise in the past and perhaps the massive profits which it expects to make in the Middle East ought to be funnelled through one of these companies which has been incurring losses in Europe. Alternatively, it may have excess scope for credit for double tax relief purposes in a country, particularly where it can carry back, and carry over, excess foreign taxes.

It will also have to consider any regulatory requirements such as the necessary profit repatriation under exchange control or possibly take a risk where it has to apply for consent prior to a foreign re-organisation and so on. It is a little pointless for a company to avoid local tax and then find that it has to bring all its profits back and pay tax in its home country anyway.

These points, and many others, may override the local tax considerations and outweigh the opportunities for mitigation. Furthermore, the constraints of local commercial law may necessitate, for example, that operations have to be carried on through a branch (possibly a branch of a Germany company, a Swiss company or maybe a United Kingdom company) and that tax planning in the Middle East is ruled out for commercial reasons.

In general terms, doing business 'with' a Middle East country does not generate local taxation liabilities unless royalty, know-how or similar payments are involved. The definition of 'with' or 'in' is very important, and local advice should be taken on this question.

For example, when goods are delivered to Saudi Arabia, if they are delivered c.i.f. to a port there, that is doing business 'with' and there is no problem; but if the goods are delivered to an inland city and the company is responsible for the freight inside Saudi Arabia, then this is doing business 'in' and can generate local tax liabilities. Those rules were promulgated in 1970 (1389 in the Islamic calendar) in the Second Circular of that year.

2—The accounting framework

Having decided to do business in the Middle East, a company will then have to consider the accounting framework, the investment restrictions and taxation in general.

Dealing with the accounting framework first, it is a requirement, for example in Iran, that companies submit annual financial statements to the Registrar and to shareholders, audited and certified principally by a member of the Chartered Institute of England & Wales, Ireland or Scotland or by a Certified Accountant.

Iraq, like other countries in the Middle East, however, has not developed a framework of generally accepted accounting principles as they are understood in either the UK or the United States. There are no bodies of the status of the professional accounting bodies in the United Kingdom, although various organisations in the countries concerned, such as the Iraqi Qualified Accountants' Society, do promote accounting principles. Some of the smaller countries such as Bahrain and Abu Dhabi do not even require the submission of financial statements, either to government agencies or to shareholders, but in general terms there is a requirement to submit financial statements to government or tax or industry agencies, as well as to shareholders.

(a) The auditor

The status of the auditor varies from country to country. In Kuwait an auditor must be an experienced graduate, and must be independent. Iran licenses official accountants whose certification is accepted by the tax authorities, unless they suspect fraud. Accounts of companies listed on the Tehran stock exchange must be certified by a company auditor and by an 'approved auditor'. Accounting policies themselves are not materially different from those in the United Kingdom, there naturally being the odd accounting quirk. Taxes are usually recorded in the books of account in the year in which the income is earned; however, refinements such as deferred tax are not customary, nor are they generally understood.

(b) Revaluation of assets

Revaluation of assets, without incurring a tax charge, is usually allowed, Iran being the exception where a charge to tax may arise, and differences between book and tax depreciation are usually to be found. Statutory books are usually prescribed although the requirement to keep them may be waived if the accounts are kept on a computer.

(c) Appropriation of profits to reserves

The most significant accounting requirement is probably that relating to reserves, since most countries stipulate that certain amounts of profits must be appropriated to reserves. This is an important consideration from the investors' point of view as it affects the amount of profit that may be remitted to the home country. In Iran, for example, 5 per cent. of after-tax profits must be appropriated to a reserve until the reserve reaches 10 per cent. of capital when the reserve normally remains untouched until liquidation. In the Lebanon the figure is 10 per cent. of net profits up to 50 per cent. of capital, but profits may be utilised to write off losses. Some countries specify a minimum investment in government bonds when a company has made profits or when it has remitted dividends; this is generally up to about 5 per cent. of profits and Egypt and Iraq both require 25 per cent. of net profit to be distributed to employees. However, in Egypt, in an attempt to encourage foreign investment, they are re-considering this 25 per cent. level.

The strict requirements of the Tehran stock exchange relating to financial statements, prospectuses and integrity of promoters, demonstrates the direction of progress of accounting principles in the Middle East. It is likely to be rapid from now on, but a lot of work is needed to standardise the customs of accounting.

3—Investments in the Middle East

(a) General

Looking at investment in the Middle East, the last few years have seen a dramatic reversal of the policy where foreign investment is concerned. Most countries are now actively in favour of foreign investment, especially of that type of investment which boosts exports or reduces their imports. Individual governments play a large role in the economy and some sectors of the economy are either closed to the private sector or open only on a joint venture basis. At the same time, however, increasing encouragement is given to the private sector.

Most countries limit the level of foreign capital participation and the upper limit is often 49 per cent. of foreign capital but it does depend on the subject matter of the contract as well as the business concerned. Instances of foreign participation as high as 90 per cent. are known, but these are generally unusual now and one is more likely to find levels of between 30 per cent. and 45 per cent. Governments are tending to be selective and investments must be in development or productive activities which are beneficial to the home economy in some way. If existing home capital and expertise are considered sufficient investments will probably not be given the necessary seal of approval.

Egypt is an example of a country where conscious efforts have been made to attract investment, for it is a country that is densely populated and rather poor compared with its neighbours. Whilst applications are necessary, once the need for the project has been established all possible assistance is forthcoming and the rules tend to be bent fairly dramatically. An agreement with Switzerland provides, for example, for the free transfer of profits and capital, with arbitration procedures in the event of investment disputes. Whilst a minority holding may not seem an attractive proposition, foreign companies now negotiate more and more management agreements which effectively keep management control and majority participation in profit in their own hands even though they may not have shareholder control.

(b) Repatriation of profits

The safety of one's investment must be one of the first considerations after establishing that such an investment is feasible. Profit and capital are generally available for repatriation subject to certain limitations, exchange control regulations and the usual administrative approval. Guarantees on repatriation are more specific and create more confidence in some countries than in others. There exists in Iran, for example, a law for the protection of foreign capital which guarantees repatriation of profits in the currency of the original investment upon submission of financial statements and evidence of payment of appropriate taxes. Most countries allow repatriation of profits subject to legal reserves but one cannot really divorce these assurances from the political situation that exists in the Middle East.

Loans usually require approval and such approval will often extend to the repayment schedule. Repatriation is, of course, subject to exchange control regulations and these regulations used to be very strict, but have now been considerably relaxed with the inflow of dollars. The problem remains, however, to some extent in Egypt and in Syria. It should be borne in mind, however, that regardless of these limits, excessive remittances of profit can incur the displeasure of government agencies. It is therefore advisable to be judicious, especially since high remittances are likely to come under increasing fire in the future.

4—The basis of company taxation

Turning to the basis of company taxation, all countries in the Middle East impose some form of tax on manufacturing and trading activities registered in the country concerned. The tax charge is generally based on income, which will be defined later, less allowable deductions. Company tax is made up of various taxes such as the basic tax, municipal tax, reconstruction tax, defence tax and, for example in Syria, a tax of 15 per cent. on rents. Temporary and permanent surcharges on tax are frequently found.

Some countries differentiate between a branch and a company; some distinguish between foreign and 'home' entities. Saudi Arabian 'home' companies, for example, only pay a voluntary Jihad tax, which is a holy war tax with graduated rates between 1 per cent. and 5 per cent. Generally, the tax morality of businessmen can be said to be fairly poor in the Middle East, although the tax administrators and judiciary are of a high standard. In Iran, for example, appeal from a tax assessor is to a Tax Assessment Commission, which is fairly high in the judicial hierarchy and complaints about the Commission are then heard by the Tax Council.

5—Taxable income and allowable expenses

Generally speaking, taxable income in the Middle East is defined as income earned in a country arising from some form of activity carried on in that country. Egypt is one country which taxes foreign source income of a local entity, but it has concluded tax treaties with a number of countries which may reduce its tax burden. Libya also taxes income derived from abroad in a number of cases. Certain income is specifically excluded from taxable income, the most significant being that excluded under the tax incentive schemes. In Egypt and Iran dividends from local companies are not taxable, otherwise nearly all forms of income and gain are brought into charge to tax. Tax-allowable deductions from gross income are, as one would expect, rent, payroll, stock, etc.; most expenses which relate directly to the earning of taxable income are allowable for tax.

(a) Depreciation

All countries allow depreciation at varying rates and these rates are often not specified in law, but are established by custom. The rates allowed do not come anywhere near the 50 per cent. and 100 per cent. available in the United Kingdom for buildings and machinery respectively. In Saudi Arabia, for example, average tax depreciation is about 10 per cent.; in Lebanon it goes from 2 per cent. to 12 per cent., but accelerated depreciation of up to 15 per cent. is available where a company does not avail itself of other tax incentives.

Reasonable royalties and management fees are generally deductible, but are often subject to withholding tax. Dividends are normally paid out of post-tax profits. Where they are deductible in arriving at taxable profits, as in Egypt, withholding tax applies. In Iraq, however, dividends are deductible and there is no withholding tax. Losses may generally be carried forward and set off against future profits. In Iraq and Libya the limit is five years; in Iran and Egypt three years. There are, however, no carry-back provisions.

(b) Expenses

The tax authorities may consider expenses to be excessive. In Iran there have been many instances where expenses have been subject to disallowance as not reasonably necessary in the production of the *relevant* incomes. The expenses susceptible to such disallowances include advertising, travel, professional fees and, obviously, Head Office allocations and charges. In the last of these, Head Office allocations, there is likely to be severe enquiry and substantial disallowance. In 1970 Saudi Arabia issued a circular stating that no expense relating to a non-taxable profit or a profit subject to tax in a previous or subsequent year is deductible, and this circular specifically disallowed any amount of the general administrative expenses spent by the main office abroad. This potential disallowance is even more swingeing than those required or presumed under the

German or French tax codes. In practice it is not quite as rigidly applied, but in theory no deduction is available for Head Office allocations or management charges. Additionally, if the Head Office disburses technical expenses which are connected with the earning of taxable profits they are only deductible on the submission of a detailed supporting statement and after long negotiations.

Obviously the tax planning problem, which is equally as applicable to all countries in the Middle East as probably to all countries in the world, is partly solved by ensuring that as much expense as possible is incurred directly in the appropriate country by the operating entity there. In short, all expenses should be charged and paid in the country. If Head Office employees are seconded to the Middle East, they should have service agreements wherever possible drawn up with the local entity and it should pay their air fares, rather than attempting to allocate them after payment in London.

(c) Royalties

It has been mentioned that royalties are normally deductible, but they frequently involve lengthy processes of authorisation and tax withholding and then negotiation as to the deductibility at the end of the day. Wherever possible, it is advisable to avoid material royalties where that cost can be included in a charge for supplies. The status of accounts for tax purposes is often unclear and, in certain areas, there is a tendency to establish taxable profits as a percentage of gross income. This can be arbitrarily assessed in Saudi Arabia—the inductive levels are between 15 per cent. and 40 per cent. of gross income. In the Lebanon the inductive rates are 15 per cent. for carpet dealers, 50 per cent. for architects and only 40 per cent. for pimps and prostitutes! In Iran and Saudi Arabia a choice exists between the arbitrary method and producing an income and expenses statement. It is necessary to be alert to taking advantage of whichever method is most beneficial to the company itself.

Take, for example, a United Kingdom company which contracts to deliver and instal equipment in Saudi Arabia. The fact that it is installing the equipment makes the company liable to Saudi tax. The arbitrary percentage method may be most beneficial, but if the company sub-contracts it would then be clearly beneficial to produce financial statements and pay taxes on the excess of income over the sub-contract costs. The final point on this particular topic is that where there is a withholding applicable to the contract, as there would be in the contract just described, it should be ensured that the contract provides for repayment of any excess tax withholding, or it may not be recoverable.

6—Tax rates

The tax rates in a number of Middle East countries are summarised in Appendix A, p. 89 , together with their basis of computation. These are provided for comparative purposes and may not reflect recent changes. This computation summary attempts to show the effective rates of tax on a given amount of income in each country. It must be appreciated that the calculations are greatly simplified and do not show the detail of the interaction of the various taxes. Taking Iran for example, the calculation does not bring out the fact that the 25 per cent. tax on retained earnings is available as a credit against withholding tax on future distributions. It is obviously impossible to take account of all possible variations and they are merely to act as a guide.

7—Tax incentives

Of greater significance to the potential investor than the company tax rates in the various countries, are those measures that provide for a degree of exemption from taxation. These exist in practically all countries to a greater or lesser degree and are of vital importance in deciding upon the structuring of proposed investments, on the return required and on the structure of international operations to make that investment. Operations may be eligible for various tax holidays and rebates, for tax exemption, duty exemptions on imported equipment and raw materials, tariff protection, government grants and possibly low cost loans. Almost invariably these incentives are granted on an individual basis on application to the appropriate authority controlling foreign investment. Applications for incentives should be incorporated into the preliminary application to set up the project and, in terms of tax, it is effectively the value of the project to the country concerned that decides the form of tax benefit that can be obtained and the type of local structure that is available.

It has already been mentioned that governments tend to be selective in their approval of investments and it will come as no surprise to find that this selectivity extends to incentives. The rule is export orientation and import substitution. Iran encourages all types of manufacturing industries, especially for building materials and the development of agriculture, whereas Lebanon is interested in textiles and electrical equipment. There are, however, other factors; Governments are concerned to decentralise industry and will encourage the location of industries away from the established industrial and commercial centres. In Iran, for example, profits of a company located more than 75 miles from Tehran will be exempt from tax for five years, whereas the exempt portion of a company's earnings within 75 miles of Tehran can be as low as 20 per cent. Indeed it is possible in some border areas to obtain a 100 per cent. exemption for a total of 12 years and profits which are invested in the production of certain goods will again be exempt from Iranian tax on retained earnings for three years. Lebanon grants a 6-year corporate income tax waiver which is extended to 10 years in the undeveloped areas. Lebanese firms not benefiting from the tax holiday can claim accelerated depreciation, i.e., raising it from 12 per cent. to perhaps 15 per cent.

Investors must be alert to any restrictions attached to the granting of favourable tax status. Restrictions are almost certain to apply according to the type of operation and its location but there may also be others. Lebanon, for example, imposes a minimum capital investment and a minimum payroll, exclusive of top salaries. Additionally, firms benefiting from tax exemptions must continue operating in the Lebanon at the end of the exemption period for as many years as the exemption was granted for. If they fail to do this they become liable for the tax waived.

A further restraint may be found in the amount of foreign investment. A ten-year tax holiday is available in certain cases in Kuwait, provided that 51 per cent. of the investment is Kuwaiti capital. Similarly, in Saudi Arabia the five-year tax exemption is only available for foreign enterprises if Saudi capital participates to the extent of at least 25 per cent. throughout the five-year period.

There may be other incentives in addition to tax incentives. Firms qualifying for incentives often do not have to pay import duties. Governments may be prepared to guarantee loans, to assist in finding land that can be used by the investing company (as well as personnel) and to speed up the administrative procedures, especially if there is a prospect of substantially increased exports. The import of competing goods may be discontinued or tariff protection may be made available to enable the company to withstand foreign competition, once the investment has been made. Finally, grants may be available—Iran has been known to provide grants ranging from 50 per cent. to 100 per cent.—for certain projects in agriculture and there may be even complete exemption from certain laws, such as the requirement in Egypt to distribute 25 per cent. of the profits to workers. With so many incentives, it is vital to research this area in some detail before making the initial application to invest. The tax burdens of a company manufacturing non-essential goods for home consumption in the suburbs of Tehran and of a company earning identical profits, situated in the border areas and exporting, are totally different.

8—Taxation of branch operations

Turning to the question of branch operations, it is often one of the prime tax considerations, when investing in a foreign country, to decide whether to operate as a branch or a locally incorporated subsidiary. This question is as applicable to the Middle East as elsewhere. It is the non-tax considerations locally involving equity participation and administrative start-up procedures that are usually the dominant factors, to a lesser extent in certain countries than in others. Firms operate a branch operation in order to avoid the equity restrictions, such as those in the Lebanon which require that 50 per cent. of the Board of Directors be Lebanese and that each director must own at least 1 per cent. of the minimum capital. In Syria, on the other hand, one might be reluctant to operate via a branch, as there is a requirement that the branch manager must be a Syrian citizen. In Egypt, Kuwait and Saudi Arabia branches are taxed in almost exactly the same manner as locally incorporated subsidiaries and consequently it is generally again the non-tax considerations which are relevant.

Tax planning becomes a slightly more important factor under the more sophisticated tax laws such as exist in Iran. In Iran a branch is taxed at the rate applicable to the withholding tax on dividends paid to a non-resident and is not subject to the company tax or the municipality tax—these are summarised in Appendix A on p. 89. A direct comparison between a branch and a company is difficult, since a company generally must be 50 per cent. Iranian owned. A branch which retains all its income may be more heavily taxed than a company retaining all its income because the company will be subject to the basic tax rates and the tax on retained earnings, whereas the branch will suffer graduated tax rates. A branch which repatriates all its income is certainly more heavily taxed than a company, but this is because, in practice, 50 per cent. of the company's distribution must go to Iranian shareholders where the withholding tax is limited to 15 per cent. Another technical consideration is that branch operating losses can be utilised immediately by the owning company whereas subsidiaries may not. That is why an investor must always look at its overall international planning in the first place and then look at the local planning possibilities later.

9—The attitude of Government agencies

Finally, the indeterminate consideration: the attitude of government agencies. Branch/Head Office relations are likely to come under greater scrutiny than parent/subsidiary ones. In the case of a subsidiary, the authorities are less inclined to disallow inter-company charges, whereas a branch's expenses arouse suspicion, especially where they are re-charged from Head Office. It may be useful to quote part of the Saudi Circular on re-charging for branch expenses. First of all, the expenses of a Saudi branch must be a real, actual, certain expenditure which must not be offset by a decrease in value of fixed assets or goods. Expenditure must be caused by the production or safeguarding of profit, and such profits must be subject to tax. The circular goes on to state: 'The taxpayer may not deduct from the proceeds of his activity in the Kingdom any amount as an indirect expense against the share of his profits or any general administrative expenses spent by his Head Office abroad, since his profits resulting from a local source within the Kingdom must be affected only by costs directly related to such profits . . .'.

(This clause presumes that a Head Office expense cannot be directly related to local profits.) The Circular goes on for another 2½ pages and the real sting is in the tail: it has retroactive effect, covering all years of assessment that were still open—in many cases, a substantial number of years.

Whilst a number of factors have to be considered when deciding if and how to operate in a Middle East country, these points cannot be considered in isolation. The final decision can only be made by the interaction of all the points discussed. One crucial factor remaining is the effect of double tax treaties. No country in the Middle East has a comprehensive tax treaty with the United Kingdom. Indeed, only two—Iran and Lebanon—have an agreement of any kind. In both cases these are limited to the agreement for avoiding double taxation on aviation profits. Some European countries do, however, have tax treaties with countries in the Middle East. Iran has a treaty with West Germany, the Lebanon has a treaty with France, and Egypt has a treaty with Italy as well as certain other European countries. The importance of a treaty, from the point of view of the investing company, principally lies in its effect on the rate of withholding tax applied by the Middle East country to dividends, royalties, management fees, and so on.

Take Egypt as an example; there the effective tax rate of 38·05 per cent. is applied to profits after deducting any dividend, but the dividend is then subject to a withholding tax of 38·05 per cent. If there was no withholding tax and the Egyptian subsidiary paid out all its profits in the form of a dividend, little tax would be incurred. In fact the treaty with Italy waives the majority of the withholding tax.

Take the case of a company in the United Kingdom wishing to do business in Iran. If it sets up a subsidiary, its dividends are subject to withholding tax at graduated rates of between 15 per cent. and 55 per cent. If the United Kingdom company were to use a West German subsidiary as an intermediary, it might be able to obtain a benefit, since under the Iran/West Germany treaty dividends are only subject to a flat 15 per cent. withholding. Whether routing dividends through West Germany could provide a benefit would depend upon total group structure and the present tax exposure of the West German subsidiary and also the UK/West Germany tax treaty.

It is fair to say that the tax laws in most countries of the Middle East are sufficiently well defined for the investor to be able to compute his tax liability with a fair degree of precision, once he has gone through the commercial negotiations and his project has been evaluated by the local country. It is also true to say that few of the laws and regulations are absolutely inviolable—the investor really needs to be aware more of the commercial, political and industrial environment than of the detailed tax provisions. In fact, no foreigner can be really aware of the detailed tax provisions in these countries.

Finally, decisions can have far-reaching implications in terms of tax and, although a company may generally employ an international tax expert to assist it, it is of vital importance that it obtains the services and assistance of a local accountant, lawyer or tax negotiator.

Questions and Answers

Question

Do you find that in many cases, taking the advice of the local tax expert who works closely with the government can be extremely helpful in dealing with rather problematical situations?

Answer

Absolutely. No person operating in a country outside the Middle East can have either the necessary expertise or the necessary knowledge of the local environment to do anything other than broadly say: 'Well, the facts are so and so, go and chat to somebody locally'. It is only in putting the package together that one needs to use an international expert.

Question

What are the essential differences in taxation for a branch of a foreign firm in Iran—for example architects or consulting engineering practices?

Answer

Architects and consulting engineering practices in Iran pay tax at the rates for branches, which are the rates from 15 per cent. to 70 per cent. and may be subject to creditable or non-creditable withholding taxes on gross income.

Question

What are the English language source materials?

Answer

There are very few that are of any value at all. Certain accountancy firms have a few publications, such as Price Waterhouse, Coopers and Arthur Andersens, which give a general background. I know that there are also English translations of four or five tax codes available—including those of Libya, Iran and Lebanon. Apart from that, one generally has to go to publications such as *Diamond's Foreign Tax and Trade Briefs* and *Tax Management International* and its associated publications.

Question

In the case of a supply contract involving a local installation whereby one is deemed as doing business 'in' that country and hence liable to local taxation, is tax applied, first to that part of the contract undertaken in the country; secondly to the whole contract; or is the application wider than that? And, as a specific example, would the sending from the United Kingdom, say, of up to six constructional supervisors or technical advisers for a construction project for up to 24 months to a Middle East country be termed doing business 'in' or 'with' that country, when there is no branch or local company established?

Answer

Almost certainly the answer to the second question is that it would be doing business 'in', although it may be possible to structure fee payments so that taxes are reduced substantially. Generally in the case of a supply contract, where a company does part of the work in and part of its work outside, there is a possibility (particularly if it is able to split its corporate entities involved) of arranging for only the work done in the country to be subject to taxation, but in this sort of area it is preferred to split contracts down amongst group companies so far as possible, so that it can be clearly established that there is no direct or indirect relationship between the business in the local country and what is done outside.

Question

Generally, does the Middle East seek to tax income from all sources worldwide, or only the income of expatriates derived from their residence in the country in question, and how long would it be before they become liable to local tax?

Answer

Generally (and this is very general, for provisions differ in almost every country), if a person is in the local country less than six months, whilst technically he has a liability to tax on the income earned whilst there, it is the income earned, including fringe benefits, whilst he is in that country, which are liable; however, fringe benefits are usually defined as X per cent. of income and housing is often deemed to be 15 per cent. of income. The majority of individuals, if they are there less than six months, perhaps escape with a lower liability than that, particularly if a person has timed his bonuses to arrive a month after he has left the local country. If a person is there more than six months, technically, in most cases, tax applies to worldwide income, although in very few cases is tax ever paid on this basis.

Question

Is there a general danger of retrospective taxation in the Middle East, and how can the effects be avoided?

Answer

There is a danger of retrospective legislation, as was evidenced by the Second Circular in Saudi Arabia in 1970 on the treatment of Head Office charges (see p. 49, *ante*). There they totally changed their stand on the deductibility of Head Office or parent company allocations of cost. This change applied to all income tax assessments which had not been finally determined as at the date of the decree, which could be very easily three or four years back. At that time, in the case of certain of the oil companies, I think it was seven or eight years back.

Question

Is there a possibility of carrying forward losses in Iran?

Answer

Yes—for up to three years.

Question

Do, first, the government and second, private companies have a right to indemnify foreign suppliers in respect of withholding and other taxes?

Answer

There is no reason why not. In most of the countries concerned it is merely a matter of contractual liability. It is like agreeing to pay an additional 10 per cent. of the price. It will probably be found that such 10 per cent. is also subject to tax, so that the grossed-up amount should be provided for in the contract.

Question

Are there any Middle East countries with no exchange control at all?

Answer

Technically, the majority. There is very free inter-changeability of money in practically all the Middle East countries. Egypt and Syria are probably the only ones that have really severe exchange control regulations.

Question

Where a company carries out its research and development in Europe and applies a recovery levy on its subsidiary in the Middle East, would this be regarded as a Head office charge?

Answer

Generally yes; the answer would be the same for levies to Germany or America, although perhaps it is even more difficult to obtain a deduction in Saudi Arabia.

The Practical Aspects of Doing Business in the Middle East

by

Nigel Spinks, LL.B.(Lond.)

Nigel Spinks is a solicitor and, in addition to having his own London practice, is a partner in the firm of Frith Kirk and Spinks, consultants in all aspects of international trade and investment, with special reference to the Middle East.

1—Introduction

When leading a Saudi trade mission to the U.K. recently, Sheikh Abdulla Alireza declared that:

> 'The objectives of Saudi investors are the industrialisation of Saudi Arabia and the professional training of its inhabitants'.

This policy statement applies not only to Saudi Arabia, but also to all the areas in the Middle East in which the foreign businessman is going to do business. It indicates the sort of contribution that is expected to be made, although it must always be remembered that this course of action means the training of potential competitors—competitors who, furthermore, will have the backing of that enormous mountain of accumulating petro-dollars and who will themselves eventually want to go offshore to areas of weak and undervalued currency and plentiful labour.

How important is it to look at alternative ways of penetrating the market? In the long-run direct investment must be more important than exporting. The value of local production abroad by, say, US-based companies is approximately six times the value of US exports and it has been increasing at the rate of 10 per cent. per year as against the 5 per cent. rate of export expansion. The total book value of all overseas direct investment throughout the world is estimated by the OECD as $90 billion; it has an estimated production value of $180 billion a year. In 1968 the value of output of US companies abroad was estimated at $120 billion. Exports from major countries were only $130 billion. An appreciation of this situation is specially relevant to the UK at the moment in that with a steadily declining currency value, acquiring production and facilities abroad has the added bonus, not merely of a return from the industrial activities, but a better return in currency terms because of the appreciation of local currencies against sterling. Such an increase shows up on the consolidated accounts but will not normally be taxable in the parent companies' hands.

2—Nature of the Middle East market

Despite the existence of the Arab League and the Council of Arabic Economic Unity, it is important to stress that the area is very far from being a common market. The Council of Arabic Economic Unity was formed in 1964 by Egypt, Iraq, Syria, Jordan and Kuwait. It has since been joined by Yemen and most recently by the Emirates.

It has permanent representatives seconded to it by the participating States, but all its resolutions are subject to ratification. Its stated objectives are to serve as a customs union and to co-ordinate economic, financial, social and labour policy. In fact, there has been a lack of economic co-ordination and the only progress so far that can be detected is that there is some degree of mutual tariff exemption which does not apply at all yet in Yemen or Kuwait. What this means is that, unlike the European Economic Community, it is not possible to be in one Arab country and be allowed to trade or have freedom of establishment in another. This is important since it means in practice that the apparently free and uncontrolled business environment in, say, the Emirates or Kuwait may not be particularly useful, since it will be necessary to deal afterwards with the distribution problems in those other countries that are in practice the market to be penetrated.

There are likely to be three possible objectives for a UK company in doing business in the Middle East. First, having expertise, a product and fully utilised facilities in its own country, it may wish simply to build a plant in order to satisfy a worldwide market and merely needs capital. The Middle East may be convenient if the added value is high in relation to transport. Second, the company may merely wish to sell UK production to the Middle East. Third, the UK company may need local production to satisfy the local market in the Middle East for reasons of distribution policy, servicing, parts supply, capital requirements and, of course, the cost of the product vis-à-vis the competitors in that market in that area.

3—Choice of system of market penetration

Against these three objectives there are perhaps five possible ways of doing business. First, there is the distributor and the agent set-up. Iraqui law, in fact, specifically provides that an agent includes a distributor, although the position in this respect varies throughout the Middle East. The second alternative is a selling subsidiary in the branch, the third licensing, the fourth the turnkey contract and the fifth, the joint venture. No mention is made of the wholly owned manufacturing company because a glance at the chart in Appendix B, p. 96 , shows that this is not really going to succeed unless one is in a free zone such as Egypt or Syria. The same principle is true for the selling subsidiary or branch and, again, if it is a wholly owned subsidiary it is going to be treated as a branch. Only in the

Lebanon, Iraq, Oman and the Emirates is a branch likely to be legally possible, and in Iraq the law states that a branch must not act as a distributor.

The straightforward licence is also unlikely merely from the nature of the situation. Because Arab countries need European know-how, it is presumably possible, and will be advantageous, to demand equity as well as royalty, but apart from this there is not yet sufficient expertise in most areas to use a licence effectively. Arab countries are unique historically in that they have cash, an expanding market, and an apple that everybody wants a bite of, but with little existing on-going manufacturing business that can be used to break into that market. To make the licence work, therefore, requires the sort of know-how commitment, training, secondment of personnel that can be associated only with joint ventures.

In practice, therefore, there are just two situations that need to be considered, the distributorship and the composite structure, the latter consisting of a corporate vehicle, a licensing and know-how contract, a turnkey contract, a supplies and/or purchase contract, all with a joint venture company.

(a) Distributorship

The main problems to think about in this connection are definition of the product line, payment, stockholding, cost of advertising, technical expertise in and knowledge of the product significant to its marketing by the agent, servicing and spares problems, Arabic labelling and the possibility of licensing trade mark rights. In addition there may also be import licensing—either direct or by way of exchange control allocations—to contend with and consideration will have to be given whether or not to have local assembling, packaging, bulk breaking or fabrication. A consideration is that there will be few, if any, anti-trust rules in the area limiting the parcelling up of markets by rival UK manufacturers. Indeed, the point has been made quite specifically that UK manufacturers should get together and trade co-operatively in the area in a way that would probably be unlawful within the Common Market or in the United States. Under English law, of course, companies are permitted to make agreements relating to exports that would otherwise be void under restrictive practices legislation.

The UK company will wish to retain as much profit as possible while at the same time giving the local agent enough cash to deal with all the problems that he faces and to motivate him to better results. The manufacturer will also wish to ensure that the goodwill his products develop in the territory will belong to him and not to his representative. The structure of the distributors' agreement will have to deal with all these issues. It is unlikely in practice that the local agent will be able to deal adequately with requirements for technical expertise and with the servicing of spares, because normally he has many product lines. It would be a problem to make him keep complete stock ranges of all models. The practical answer to this may be either to second employees to the agent or to set up a servicing and/or stockholding company according to the joint venture rules, which will be dealt with later, on p. 69.

Manufacturers are nearly always sceptical of the technical competence of their agents and it is beyond dispute that in the Middle East agents with employees who fully understand the products are going to be hard to find. The foreign manufacturer must understand that his role is not to be critical but to solve the problem by active education and concern. By this type of activity, he will motivate the local people and find it easier to obtain the official consents he will need to set up more elaborate operations later on. A manufacturer needs local people on his side:

(i) to plug him into the local distribution system;

(ii) to obtain premises and labour; and

(iii) to secure the goodwill of local officialdom.

In fact, local rules are perhaps not so difficult as they may seem. In Abu Dhabi, for instance, the law says that 25 per cent. of the profit from trading operation must go into the hands of a local participant. In practice, however, a side agreement provides for a pay-back of perhaps some of this profit to the foreign trader by way of commissions or fees. If there is any problem in enforcing this side agreement, the Shari'a court will first impose a fine for being in breach of the trading regulations; the court will then enforce the side agreement as a contract between the parties. It might, however, be stretching the possibilities of the situation a little too far if an attempt is made to use a local national as a mere nominee.

In some countries the major buyers will be the government or its agencies. Many countries require tender documents which must be submitted through a local agent and performance bonds or bank guarantees will often be demanded. In Syria, for instance, the private importer has also become non-existent and, although there is some current revival in this sector for substantial business, the foreign exporter must in practice sell to one of the five state importers. Direct investments are going to be impossible there, except by going into a free zone and the Syrian policy is to buy know-how and contract for cash, rather than for equity which would be held by foreigners.

A good distributorship contract should therefore first define (i) the area and the degree of exclusivity and (ii) the relationships with agents or distributors in other territories. Second, it should specify prices, commissions, margins, discounts as against volume, and the basis of purchase (i.e., c.i.f. or whatever) and should deal with the provision for variation of prices. Third, it should provide for a call-off mechanism, a method of payment (letters of credit or whatever) and should provide also for the currency in which prices are going to be stipulated. One small point worthy of mention is that if a manufacturer sells into Libya, the Libyan authorities insist that the insurance on transport into Libya must be Libyan insurance, and therefore the manufacturer can sell to Libya only on a c. *and* f. basis and not c.i.f.

Stock levels are an important factor in profitability, for delivery on consignment is not normally going to be practicable, so some way should be thought of to make sure that the distributors hold commercially adequate levels of stocks. This means that the distributor will require protection against price reduction and obsolescence.

The distributor must be made responsible for obtaining all necessary licences and foreign exchange consents from the governments of the countries in which he is trading and must procure Arabic translations of trade marks and trade literature. Finally, the agreement must provide for advertising and promotion costs and efforts, resale price maintenance, feed-back of marketing information, the termination of the agreement and disposal of stocks then held, and non-competition clauses.

Trade mark expenditure should not be spared. Although there is a paragraph in all Department of Trade booklets that British companies are advised to register their trade marks and patents, the protection of trade marks in this area really can be important. In an expanding market of this size, there is ample scope for piracy of marks. In any situation where agents hold large stocks of competing product lines, the time probably comes when they want to be rid of them at any price on a job lot basis when, no doubt, a certain amount of relabelling will take place.

Additionally, in a situation where selling is carried on through distributors who do carry large stocks of various lines of products, having a really well protected, distinctive and known trade mark does give the manufacturer some individuality and makes the goods more saleable at the right price and therefore more interesting to the distributor. Where there is no official trade mark registration, as in Saudi Arabia or the Emirates, a notice of ownership should be published in both scripts if it is a word mark. This will give some protection, since Shari'a courts are influenced by both fairness and good international practice.

As a contract, an arrangement with a local agent/distributor is unlikely to pose any special problems under local laws other than in such areas as licensing, control of imports and access to currency. It is possible, of course, to make contracts subject to English Law, but for them to be enforceable out there, this may not in practice go very far; in reality local courts are going to apply local law anyway.

(b) The composite arrangement

A composite arrangement will comprise a master agreement, and stemming from it, details as to the company structure, licences for patents, trade marks, copyright and know-how, a material or parts supply contract, perhaps a turnkey contract and possibly a re-purchase and distributorship contract for sales in third countries.

In this context, before looking at the corporate aspects of such transactions, the question of confidentiality ought to be given some consideration. This involves not only the possibility of the corporate misuse of information, but dissemination through the mobility of employees. Given the general objectives of Arab investors that this chapter began with, how do local laws deal with this problem? The protection of inventive technology by patents will not always be possible in the area. The chart in Appendix B on p. 96 shows that some countries do not have a formal patent law and that, generally speaking, those that do are not members of an international convention. This creates considerable difficulty in relation to priority and novelty; the expense of taking effective protection throughout the area would be very high. Decisions to spend on patent protection in any event would always have to be taken before the commercial value or effectiveness of an invention is apparent.

In the absence of patent or effective copyright law or protection, the position of know-how is likely, in practice to be very much the same as it is in the United Kingdom. An unfair restraint on competition or employment is likely to be unenforceable while the type of restriction considered reasonable by international business practice would be acceptable and upheld. Care should, however, be taken to label information as confidential, and, so far as possible, to write the foreign company's own legal system into the contract under which it is disclosed by setting out the rules which in the United Kingdom would be implied. Indeed, the use of elaborate contractual provisions to make up for the absence of statutory regulations or implied terms is important, particularly the defining of accountancy arrangements for determining sales and profit figures.

In most jurisdictions the whole arrangement would generally, directly or indirectly, be subject to government supervision, so as to ensure equity for local interests, and it is not possible to rely on *Salomon* v. *Salomon* to keep the corporate veil tightly drawn between one section of the company and another. Further, it will nearly always be impossible for the joint company or the foreign partner in that joint company to own land. Muslim customary law does not recognise associations as individuals, and, in the absence of a law authorising incorporation, they cannot be formed under process of law. In fact, laws relating to companies do exist in every jurisdiction except the Emirates.

4—Company law in Iran, Dubai and Saudi Arabia

Iran, Dubai in the Emirates and Saudi Arabia provide three useful examples of the development of company law in the area and the way companies adapt to the rules applicable to foreign investors and joint ventures. There are special rules for banks, insurance and oil companies which are not discussed here.

(a) Iran

Iran has a company law enacted in 1931, that was revised in 1969, which distinguishes between public and private companies. Companies need two members, and a wholly owned subsidiary would be considered a branch. The Sherkat Sahami (the joint stock company) is most used by foreign investors. The structure of this type of company is similar to that in the United Kingdom, with management by a board having powers delegated from the members. There are provisions protecting the rights of the minority shareholders and heavy penalties for defaulting directors.

Before foreign capital can be imported, the foreign company will need a licence under the Law for the Attraction and Protection of Foreign Investment of 1955. This establishes a Board for the Attraction and Protection of Foreign Investment whose policy is to press for holdings greater than 50 per cent. for nationals. The application is made to a Centre who give a report and recommendation to the Board. The application should, in practice, disclose all associated arrangements that make up the joint venture composite deal. The emphasis on approval has shifted from import substitution to export expansion with the means of acquiring new technology for Iran.

A licence under the 1955 Act carries with it freedom from a 1 per cent. registration fee on application for foreign exchange, but to get further tax and import duty concessions the Iranian stake must exceed 60 per cent., although there have been exceptions to this, particularly where the industry was one that Iran particularly wanted to set up. A further hazard for the foreigner is the Profit Sharing Act of 1964, which provides for collective bargaining, supervised by the Ministry of Labour. Employees must get a share in profits based on productivity, length of service and wages. There are likely to be further developments in this area.

Companies must keep accounts in Farsi and these consist of journals, ledger, inventory and copy book. Accounts must be published annually. Approval under the 1955 Act carries a repatriation guarantee and gives consent to remit dividends and royalties, provided that in the former case the accounts demonstrate that adequate profits are available.

These arrangements are conditional upon the availability of currency but if it is not available, then goods can be exported without payment, free of charge. A difficulty here is the extent to which non-cash consideration for the issue of shares in an Iranian company can be deemed to be foreign capital for the purposes of that 1955 Act. The law refers only to patent rights, plant, machinery and to certain salaries, as ranking as foreign capital. It does not refer to know-how and design, and if this is not considered to be foreign capital, then there may not be any automatic dividend of repatriation right in respect of that capital. In any event any such consideration other than cash will have to be formally valued.

Licensing, turnkey and supply contracts do not provide any special difficulty beyond the necessity of presenting for approval a deal that has had the right cosmetic treatment and that can be demonstrated to be in Iran's interests. Clearly Iran will be interested in arrangements for the re-purchase of any Iranian product for export and distribution abroad to the foreign partner. It should, in practice, be difficult for the government to police transfer prices but it must be remembered that the foreign company will not normally have a majority interest on becoming a joint venture, although of course it may have effective day to day control under a management contract.

(b) Dubai

Dubai is one of the United Arab Emirates (formerly the Trucial States) and is thus a state within a federal structure. It has a widespread re-export trade to Iran and other countries to the north. In terms of commercial infrastructure and the experience of its local businessmen, Dubai is probably the place that is most usually recommended as a site for Middle East representation. It has no company law. It is unusual in that a foreign company may set up a branch there without a partner, although it cannot without consent take over an agency owned by a Dubai national. A foreign company wanting to do this must first obtain a trading licence which is issued on:

(i) the production of a local guarantee of 100,000 Dirhams (which is about £11,000). Such a guarantee normally involves a fee of 1 per cent. Lawyers and accountants, however, do not need this. Guarantees are not requested from 'international companies',

(ii) obtaining a lease for local premises;

(iii) an undertaking not to attempt in any circumstances to take over any agency which already has a representative in Dubai, and to refrain from attempting to undertake the importation or handling of goods already represented in Dubai.

A branch of a foreign company must join the Chamber of Commerce by whom it is recommended to use a local agent. It may therefore have no effective choice of local associate, if its goods have been already traded in Dubai, through an existing agent. It is usually advisable for a national to be included as a minority partner for the following reasons:

(i) a good partner can be secured before it becomes compulsory to do so and they are all fully engaged with competitors;

(ii) the terms can be freely negotiated now, but when they are stipulated by law, they may become penal;

(iii) municipal approvals will be speeded up with a national as a partner, as no doubt will other approvals later;

(iv) a suitably chosen national partner will facilitate obtaining the lease needed.

A company would, in fact, be the most satisfactory way of taking a partner and in the absence of a Dubai company law it is formed by charter. A draft charter or articles of association are submitted (in English) for the ruler's inspection. If it is intended to issue shares, for non-cash consideration, then it would be as well to provide for this in the Articles and to support the draft with a draft contract for the transfer of assets and know-how. In the chart in Appendix B, on p. 96, reference is made to 25 per cent. of profits in the Emirates going to a local partner. This is actually the situation in Abu Dhabi and not in Dubai; it is reported that the government in Abu Dhabi are becoming much more difficult about approval and generally much more participative on planning matters. In fact, it is understood that substantial relocation of industry in Abu Dhabi is being pressed for by the government there, and that some companies have been given notice to quit their premises.

There will be little point in setting up a joint venture in Dubai merely for that market alone. Licences should therefore cover the intended market areas and the agreement structure in this case should also extend to the distribution system in these areas. A decision to go to Dubai should therefore balance absence of taxes and free convertibility against import duties and the cost of separate distribution networks in other countries in the area.

In practice, one of the most useful purposes of a Dubai establishment will be the location of a marketing and distributor supervision capability, using Dubai as a centre for monitoring the sales efforts of distributors throughout the Gulf area, servicing customers and co-ordinating, but not actually handling, goods.

There is no patent or trade mark law in the Emirates, although one is being prepared in Dubai. The practice is to advertise a cautionary notice of ownership of the invention or mark. The effect of this would be to put a competitor on notice as to ownership and so put a pirate in a position of competing unfairly. A Shari'a court would proceed against such an infringer, but clearly one cannot expect the niceties of argument over the precise phraseology of patent claims that a Court of Chancery would expect in the UK.

(c) Saudi Arabia

Saudi Arabia is obviously one of the most interesting countries in the area in terms of wealth, markets and infrastructure. One is struck on looking through the legal documentation of Saudi Arabia by the sophistication of its approach. Indeed, its company law is in some ways more modern and appropriate to business life than that of the United Kingdom.

Companies are formed by registration leading to the issue of a licence and prior payment up of the capital for the issue of the shares. There is no restriction on the proportion of capital which can be allotted to a foreign company but before local production facilities can be set up the investment must be approved by the foreign investment committee of the Ministry of Commerce and Industry and receive a licence to manufacture. This committee is made up of representatives of other Ministries and a legal adviser; it also hears expert evidence. The form which must be filled in to make the application is far-reaching, and although it asks questions whose answers intending investors ought to know already, setting out the information in the manner required may be somewhat inconvenient. Details as to capital, type and amount of goods to be produced, raw materials and labour requirements, and proposed production methods, *inter alia*, must be given in this form.

The form does not, in terms, call for details of supporting arrangements but the information given will not really make sense unless full disclosure is made. In any event the Committee has power to call for such additional information as it thinks fit. Article 8 of the law of 1964 provides that the resulting company shall have all the privileges enjoyed by national capital under the National Industries Protection and Encouragement Regulations as well as exemption of the whole project from income and company taxes for five years provided Saudi interests have 25 per cent. or more of the capital. This proportion must be maintained throughout the whole period of the exemption. When the tax holiday terminates only the profits attributable to the foreign held shares are taxed, as Saudi nationals do not pay income tax. An interesting result of this considerably ameliorates the effect of giving up equity to local interests. In the absence of a full pay-out of profits (which the foreign investor is unlikely to want, since dividends will be the least attractive method of re-cycling profits), the retention of over 25 per cent. of the profits tax free effectively gives the benefit of up to 75 per cent. of the tax saved to the foreign majority.

Further advantages flowing from the approval of the investment are:

(i) capacity to own land both for industrial and residential purposes, subject to consent;

(ii) no exchange control limitations or withholding taxes;

(iii) the possibility of taking 10-year government leases at a nominal rent;

(iv) tariff and dumping protection; and

(v) acceptance by the government of a locally based tender for official contracts up to 10 per cent. higher than the lowest bid from abroad.

Theoretically, the company must employ 75 per cent. Saudis representing 51 per cent. of the value of the payroll. In practice, local labour is in short supply and wage rates are higher than elsewhere in the Middle East. Labour laws also call for social security contributions of 10 per cent. of payroll (plus 5 per cent. from the employee) and for provision of services and housing. Although the Board of the company does not need to have Saudi representatives, a foreign investor would be most unwise to go ahead without this. Care must also be taken in selecting the foreign representatives.

Article 9 of the Foreign Investment Rules prohibits persons in charge of permitted projects from concerning themselves in any way with the religious or political affairs of Saudi Arabia. Breach of this (and, of course, other) regulations can lead to the withdrawal of the manufacturing licence and the liquidation of the project.

The licence and turnkey contracts will not present any special difficulties beyond those discussed earlier in general terms, i.e., the necessity for writing a much fuller contract in the absence of terms or practices implied by law. It will also, of course, be necessary to convince the Committee that all is fair, reasonable and beneficial to Saudi Arabia. The most noteworthy problem is the absence of local patent and copyright laws. As in Dubai, a cautionary notice of ownership is published by the Ministry of Commerce and the licence will then carry such rights as this notice conveys; it will therefore be substantially a licence of know-how. In Dubai in the Emirates, where the local market is less important from the entrepreneurial aspect, this may not matter too much. In Saudi Arabia it means that great importance must be placed on the confidentiality of terms of the licence. Trade marks are registrable, and there is a difference of opinion here between the author and the booklet issued by the Department of Trade. This latter states that trade marks only last for one year; the author submits that they last for 15 years. The correct position, probably, is that they require annual renewal, but that they expire totally at the end of 15 years. There seems to be no difficulty in treating a package of quasi-patents, trade marks and know-how as foreign capital or as consideration for an issue of shares, provided, of course, the Committee find the whole project acceptable.

5—Free zone legislation in Egypt

The free zone legislation in Egypt is based on the comparatively recent law of 9th June, 1974. It sets up free zones for industrialisation under a board which is given the job of managing the zone. Subject to approval by this board, any company going into the zone can be 100 per cent. foreign owned, provided it is concerned with industrialisation, mining, energy, tourism, transport, storage, packaging, reclamation and housing—a fairly comprehensive list. There must be some profit distribution to workers, but companies are exempt from Egyptian regulations on workers' participation. Free zone companies have a tax holiday for five years from start-off of production which may be increased to eight years with approval and are free of licensing and exchange control constraints. They are, however, treated as overseas companies when selling into Egyptian markets; at that point, therefore, they are subject to Egyptian control on the licensing of imports.

6—Joint ventures generally

Apart from the points discussed in relation to specific countries, thought should be given to incorporating details of the following into joint venture and licensing agreements:

(a) Voting rights
It should be agreed which of the participants is to have entrenched rights and in which part of which agreement clauses relating to voting are to be inserted.

(b) Capital

Decisions should be made on the control over capital increases as a means of avoiding dilution. Procedures should be agreed for the transfer of shares. Rather than get involved in valuations, the author prefers the two-way option method of doing this, whereby Partner A offers to Partner B at a price and Partner B can, if he elects, buy at that price rather than sell. Detailed thought and bargaining will be necessary in relation to financing arrangements; source of funds and gearing; convertible securities; loan agreeements; preferred shares and dividend policy.

On this last point there is a peculiarity about Saudi Arabia in that Article 127 of its Companies Act states that the proportion of net profit to be distributed is to be specified in the Articles. In effect, therefore, a company does not declare a dividend in Saudi Arabia; it really decides whether to distribute or not. If it decides to distribute, then that proportion fixed in the Article is distributed, unless perhaps the company wants to amend the Articles of Association every year, which might be a problem. In practice it might give rise to a certain number of difficulties.

(c) Management arrangements

Management contracts and fees to be payable for management are, of course, a way for a foreign company to keep management control over the joint venture and possibly to cream off some of the profits by way of commissions or management fees on a continuing basis. In the absence of such arrangements the composition and replacement of the Board must be dovetailed with the voting position. The rules for the removal of directors in the jurisdiction in question must be carefully considered.

(d) Expansion

The question of expansion into other areas should be negotiated. This comes back to an earlier point—the company is training competitors and the time is going to come, certainly, when the joint venture company is going to want the right to trade into a third territory in competition with its foreign parent and it may not be possible to avoid this just by refusing to grant a license under existing patents.

(e) Procurement policies

If the local partner is to supply labour or management it must be spelt out whether this is to be on secondment, by transfer, by sub-contract or by new employment. For the sub-contract, rates must be established, as indeed must a system for the calculation of transfer prices on raw materials, finished goods for distribution or services from the foreign investor.

(f) Injection of know-how

In a composite patent, trade mark and know-how licence, the transfer of know-how for cash or shares must be considered, and whether it is to be exclusive, non-exclusive, or sold outright for a cash sum. The importance of establishing confidentiality in the absence of patent and copyright laws has already been discussed but policy decisions must be taken on associated matters such as the feedback and relicensing of improvements. The licensor must decide if he wants a club with a number of licensees in various territories who will all be feeding back information which will be re-cycled through the licensed companies. If the feedback of information is to be on an exclusive basis and the licensed company is not a subsidiary, problems may be encountered with the EEC competition laws. The EEC will normally insist on an EEC-based company taking feedback information on a non-exclusive basis so that the non-EEC company is free to licence or disclose to other EEC companies. Another extremely difficult topic is infringement by outsiders. In practice the difficulty in the Middle East is likely to stem from the lack of protection arising specifically under the law. Unless bad faith or breach of confidentiality can be shown the copyist may not be restrainable. In these circumstances the loading of a price by the imposition of a royalty may lead to a non-competitive position as against a non-royalty paying pirate. It may, therefore, be preferable to transfer the know-how involved as against a cash sum or equity share in the joint venture company and forget about third party infringement as a difficulty between the parties.

(g) Termination

The joint venture corporate structure will be indefinite with provisions enabling the exit of either side already discussed (see (b) above). The supporting agreements will have terminal dates and it may be in the interests of the foreign investor to be bought out if his management contract is deficient or purchases of material levels do not come up to the anticipated volume. The question of exit for both sides should always be most carefully negotiated in the light of local laws concerning repatriation of capital gains taxes and the treatment of surpluses arising on liquidations.

7—The role of the lawyer

Too many publications deal with what the industrialist ought to do and unsufficient attention is paid to what the lawyer can do. The lawyer's tasks, in doing business in this area, are fourfold. First, he has to advise and inform his client (and this is true whether he is an in-house lawyer or an outside consultant) so that the commercial decisions and the commercial approach, can be formulated. This will involve discussions with the local profession. Then his task is to achieve certainty, so that the commercial decisions can take effect in the way envisaged by the person taking commercial responsibility in the investing company. His next role is one of planning the structure of the transaction and its documentation in a way that is going to put the commercial decision into effect so that it optimises the benefit to his client, the participant. And finally, a somewhat new, but nevertheless important function for lawyers, is that of being almost a commercial public relations figure. In this connection, the lawyer ought to be responsible for the cosmetic presentation of plans and proposals to licensing authorities and planning boards of government authorities. The lawyer must learn to understand what governments expect and see not only that those needs are met but that also they are seen to be met. It is not enough to prepare proposals and incorporate them, the lawyer must make sure they are properly documented financially, from both a market and economic standpoint. He must ensure that appropriate local spokesmen are properly briefed and that nothing in the documentation can be lifted out of context by, perhaps, a hostile Press.

8—Future developments

The nearest parallel, historically, in recent history is Japan. Although Japan is a uniform market, it has learnt to accept foreign investment but has made it conform to rigorous rules. The Arab countries must soon develop a homogeneous approach, their own co-ordinated Ministries of International Trade and Fair Trade Commissions. They will want, soon, to take their new technologies out into the world from where they came. In Japan there were tremendous benefits for those who went into the country early, before the control system became sophisticated and effectual. Today, new investments and projects in Japan occur only where Japanese industries are prepared to tolerate them. The same is bound to occur, in time, in the Middle East.

The Legal Environment for Negotiating Commercial Agreements in the Middle East

Sami D. El-Falahi,
M.A. (Oxon), M.Sc. (Econ.), F. Inst. Pet.,
F.C.I., F.I. Arb., Barrister

Sami El-Falahi has occupied senior positions in the oil industry for some years, mainly operating in the negotiating, legal and research fields. He now works as consultant to certain international and Government companies, operating in the Middle East. He used to lecture on the legal aspects of the oil industry at Loughborough University and is now a member of the Panel of Lecturers of the Institute of Petroleum in London.

A—INTRODUCTION

1—Historical development

Any study or approach to Middle East business is never complete without first directing attention towards the historical development of the area as a whole.

The Middle East is a peculiar area on the map. It is peculiar geographically in that all through its history it has been at the intersection of all trade routes and in the way of commercial, political and social intercourse of the world. At the same time it contains the territories of Mesopotamia, now called Iraq, and the Nile, which have developed and established their own legal systems within their particular societies. To this must be added, later in history, the rather unusual incident of having all the three major religions born in the same area and, indeed, more or less in the same locality.

These basic factors combined to condition the minds of the people of that area to certain attitudes and to a certain approach towards solving problems generally in life and these problems were invariably connected either with their relationship with each other, whether socially or legally, or with the Ruler. We are here concerned with the former, not the latter.

The ancient codes of Mesopotamia, which were utterly ruthless and, to our modern attitudes, even somewhat barbaric, were at that time a great novelty. They introduced the order required in that society to govern various relationships. Those strict legal principles, which leave no place in them for negligence, or for *mens rea*, or for any general intention of the party, have affected practically all the succeeding generations in the area. In fact, some of those principles were also apparent in the modern religions which have, since their birth, affected not only this area, but also the whole world. Interestingly, while Christianity seemed to develop geographically on a vertical line, towards Europe and above, Islam developed in a horizontal way towards Africa, Asia and China. But the centre of those two lines is the centre of the Middle East. Thus the Middle East has been, in a sense, the forum where all the ideas of the various religions and civilizations have been interacting to produce the attitudes and characteristics witnessed in the area in the 1970s.

The surprising degree of pragmatism seen in commercial negotiations and business transactions, presents a puzzle to the outsider when compared with the Arab's deep rooted belief in the non-material and his total surrender to certain conceptual ideals such as honour and fate.

This combination (or contradiction as some Western observers have described it) can be simply explained by the unwavering pride of the people of the area in their past history and their present deep feeling of exasperation at having been 'left behind' in the modern, highly technical world we live in.

The sooner the foreign businessman realises and comprehends this, the easier it will be for him to tackle this 'strange' mixture of contradictions.

2—Present day developments

At the turn of this century when most of the Middle East was ruled by the Turks—who were, after all, Muslims like the majority of locals—the people of the area, to the surprise of many, sided with the British and the French and their Allies. The deep feeling of exasperation just mentioned displayed itself in a dramatic way.

But, by the end of the war, this area was divided among the victors and the influence of that division is still evident as far as the legal framework in the area is concerned. Iraq, Kuwait and the Gulf, for instance, are still very much influenced by English principles of law, while Syria, the Lebanon and Algeria are very much affected by French doctrines and legal principles.

However, soon afterwards the sudden importation of whole systems of laws was replaced by codes and laws re-embodying many of the ideals and principles cherished by the Arabs, and blended with varieties of French and English legal forms and substances, to suit the local climates and conditions.

In the period immediately after the war, the area was more or less barren; it had no major development or clearly defined economic planning. However, the big powers who emerged victorious after the First World War started to look towards this area as a field for their industrial activities and for the application of their technological skills. This, of necessity, introduced what is now known as the large government-sponsored company from the Western world.

This trend began with Great Britain, France and at a somewhat later stage, the United States. For various reasons, the agreements made by these international companies were of a peculiar nature in that they tended to offer more privileged concessions than ordinary business agreements. They involved huge areas and were made to last for a considerable number of years—some of them for 75 years. They were all connected with mineral resources, a wealth that is, by its nature, a depleting asset.

During, and immediately after, the Second World War little development took place in the area. And, indeed, for about five years after the war, there was little activity by way of promoting overseas activities in the area or in the way of negotiating, amending or modifying the existing agreements at the time. But in the early 1950s a radical change occurred and in Persia (Iran) attempts were made to nationalise the country's oil resources. This was a turning point in that it affected not only the relationship between the oil companies and the Middle East, but the relationship between all overseas companies and the people in the area, and their governments.

Defects began to be found in existing agreements and demands for change of varying degrees became the order of the day. The foreign companies, realising the changed times and moods, took the first major initiative.

(a) The profit-sharing agreement

This initiative led very quickly to two important and simultaneous developments. The first of these was the complete revision of the agreements in the area. Negotiations were started in various parts of the Middle East to bring the oil concessions up to date, and to introduce some radical changes which, only a few years previously, would have been quite unthinkable. 1952 saw the birth of the profit-sharing agreement in the area, which introduced with it a new concept—that the countries themselves should have a say, not merely in receiving royalties, but also in the structure of the agreements themselves. The idea behind this was that if partners share the profits, they must have full access to all accounts and to details of how that company's profits are made up. This change brought in its wake the idea of participation, and participation, in its turn, brought with it the idea of equality and fair play.

In addition, the profit-sharing agreement resulted in the second of the two major developments—a sudden surge of high incomes into the countries of the area.

The major agreements had been based on the system of royalties. These were fixed at a certain amount (in the case of oil production four shillings per ton produced and exported by the host country). Thus the income a host country received was dependent on the size of the production for any particular year. This fixed sum was small compared to the profits made by the companies from the same number of tons produced.

Under the new system of profit-sharing agreements, the income suddenly increased many times. Some countries' finance increased over thirty times. This surge of money into the area produced in the early 'Fifties, what we are in fact witnessing again in the early 'Seventies.

(b) The joint venture

The relationship with the foreign investor rapidly began to be seen in a different light. Thus towards the end of the 'Fifties, the idea of the joint venture, basically an American concept, was introduced.

The concept involves both parties, foreign and local, not only in the benefits accrued but also in the risk involved.

The Middle East countries proved reluctant to accept the risk element and so the joint venture agreement never really established itself. It was soon replaced by what has come to be known as the service contract.

(c) The service contract

Under this, the host country provides varying degrees of financial requirements while the incoming company provides everything else from expertise and technological know-how to training nationals and providing ancillary services and marketing.

The service contract proved to be a most attractive arrangement. It provided the foreign company with what it needed by way of goods, materials and expansion, and at the same time the pride and sovereignty of the host country were preserved.

But as the number of these contracts increased, it was immediately realised in the host country that it was more expedient to have a central body to deal with the major contracts of this or similar type. As a result, national companies or agencies began to be created as specialised bodies to handle such contracts and agreements.

(d) Investment and know-how contracts

Although the changes discussed above have been more or less connected exclusively with large contracts where the governments are themselves parties, the same principles and ideas apply by and large to agreements with individuals and smaller companies.

From the writer's experience, when a company representative negotiates in the Middle East, hc somehow begins to sense that the negotiators on the other side seem to draw a distinction between two types of agreement.

The first can be called the direct investment agreement, where the overseas company is involved in everything from skill to finance and so on and the only interest that the host country has in the agreement is either in the sharing of the profits or in the training of skills, and similar benefits. In other words the whole liability is on the incoming company. Such agreements are now almost exclusively with governments and are of substantial nature.

The second type of agreement is that which is concerned with the comparatively small scale importation of skill and expertise or goods.

This distinction is really the main influence affecting the attitude of businessmen or government departments in the area to the various types of contracts negotiated.

The difference of approach to these two categories is quite clear in many respects. For instance, in the first type of contract, the direct investment agreement, of necessity, a considerable time span is covered, probably a huge area, and quite often a considerable amount of money involving many hundreds of people. Invariably the local party here is the government or one of its departments. As this type of agreement is normally of substantial national significance, the government may overlook certain aspects of its sovereignty or may concede certain points such as accepting international arbitration or giving the foreign concern special exemptions. These privileges are seen as worthwhile compared to the great benefit to be expected from that project for the country as a whole.

In the case of the other category of agreement, such as the ordinary agreement to import say, cars, such exemptions and privileges are hardly to be expected.

B. THE LEGAL UNITY OF THE AREA

So far we have treated the area of the Middle East as a single unit, which may give the impression that exactly similar legal principles apply in all its parts. This is not so. There are important variations and these are important to consider when dealing with the various countries of the area.

For instance while in Egypt agents are not allowed to operate, except if they are state-owned trading companies, in Libya, by virtue of the Commercial Agencies Rule of 1971 and the Regulations attached thereto, individuals may act as agents so long as they hold Libyan nationality.

With respect to companies or firms operating as agents, we find that in Kuwait this is allowed by Law No. 36 of 1964, so long as ownership is at least 51 per cent. Kuwaiti, whereas in Libya, a company operating as an agent must be wholly owned by Libyans. Yet in Iran there are no specific laws regarding agencies and one has therefore to fall back on the general commercial laws of the country. In Iraq, however, Law No. 208 of 1969 allows not only Iraqis to become agents but also nationals of other Arab countries.

1—Negotiations of agreements

(a) Preparing a draft

The first point is the question of starting negotiations. Countries in the area, when they are interested in making a certain commercial venture, agreement or whatever, attach importance to speed. Speed is of the essence of the contract. One of the best ways of ensuring this is to go to the country itself with a complete draft and detailed knowledge of the background to the negotiations.

This is very important for two reasons. Submitting a comprehensive draft shows serious preliminary study of that country's requirement. This will (or should) naturally lead to a more favourable hearing. Secondly the draft itself, by becoming the basis upon which negotiations will be commenced, will save considerable time at the outset.

Drafts may embody any principle the company desires, but at all costs, they must avoid embodying a provision which does not fall within the requirements of local laws. This will give the impression that the company is either ignorant of local conditions (a bad start) or that the Company is seeking special exemptions for local laws which is normally unacceptable, as we have seen above.

(b) Clarity of agreements

One of the major problems which affect the relationship between the foreign company and the countries in the Middle East is the question of the clarity and the comprehensiveness of any agreement made. It is always advisable with a new agreement to take pains to be clear on every possible point and every conceivable aspect of the work to be undertaken. It is not a good idea to negotiate on the basis of a contract expressed in general terms, and hoping for the best if problems arise.

Courts in the Middle East will invariably interpret the contract against those who have drafted it. The *contra preferentem* rule is as popular there as it is in the United Kingdom, for example.

Clarity quite often entails producing a longer and more detailed text and should never be for sacrificed in favour of brevity.

(c) Training of nationals

The training of nationals is one of the most important aspects of any contract of substance signed with any of the countries in the area in question, and negotiators will find that this is always in the back of the local negotiators' minds.

It cannot be overemphasised that any training provision embodied in a contract submitted in the area, will very much boost such a contract which will then a have greater chance of success. This applies equally to large and small scale operations.

Even training one or two supervisors back in London or elsewhere will be a great asset to the success of the overseas company in its negotiation.

(d) Arbitration clauses and disputes

Overseas businessmen are more apprehensive of solving possible disputes in the Middle East than of any other aspect of their work there. This apprehension may be justified in certain cases, but not in the majority of them.

The basic principle in the area is that the contract is the 'law' between the parties. Therefore the foreign party in cases of disputes is held strictly to the contract he has signed. Thus if the contract has a provision for arbitration, this will be recognised and respected.

What was said about the clarity and comprehensiveness of the contract submitted applies with equal force to the provision of appropriate arbitration. Therefore, a company which has a comprehensive, well drafted arbitration clause, will be a lot better placed than one which has incorporated a generally worded provision for an arbitration clause such as 'an arbitration clause to be agreed' or 'a suitable arbitration clause', and so on.

However, before an arbitration clause is drafted, it is imperative that the local legal provisions regarding arbitration and settlement of disputes are studied so that the clause conforms to the local legal requirements. This is important because if part of the provision embodied in the contract does not conform to the local requirements, the whole provision may well fail.

It must be admitted however that recognition of an arbitration clause is not as fully respected by the courts in the Middle East as it is in this country. This can be illustrated by the fact that even if a point relating to the arbitration clause has to go to a local court either for interpretation or advice or opinion, it is more likely than not, that the court will insist on studying the whole text and not confine itself to the point submitted.

The other aspects of the arbitration clause, such as the appointment of arbitrators or umpires, must be given careful consideration. The problems faced in the United Kingdom over this is not without parallel in the area. It is surprising how some problems may arise in this respect even in important agreements. A cautionary example of the results of an ill-conceived arbitration clause can be seen in the case in 1974 of an international Pakistani company where the arbitration clause agreed between the parties provided that in cases of disputes the arbitrator should be appointed by the Confederation of British Industries; an actual dispute arose and was referred to the Confederation of British Industries. It turned out this body has no authority to intervene in such a dispute.

(e) Force majeure clauses

Another aspect of the contract to be considered is the question of force majeure clauses. These are normally considerably wider than the English Act of God concept, and it is necessary to bear two points in mind. First, the scope of the clause and the circumstances under which it will be operating, because after all that scope will be the extent to which a company will be confined in the event of some future detriment happening. The second point is to establish the position of the company in such an event.

It is obviously impossible to forsee all future contingencies, but the drafting must be based on clearly defined lines to avoid serious consequences.

Questions and Answers

Question

Is it true to say that in Iraq a distributor is by law also considered as an agent? If so, are the obstacles in Iraq in getting rid of an agent similar to those found in the Lebanon?

Answer

Normally, the term 'agent' includes a distributor and as it is put in rather a general form it is likely that this would be in practice the interpretation of this term.

In Libya this is expressly so under the Commercial Agencies Law of 1971. Moreover, in Iraq, the law allows not only Iraqis to be agents but also nationals of other Arab countries.

There is also in Iraq an investment law whereby overseas companies are encouraged to have local agents or representatives, and whatever the name given to them, in practice, it will be found that they may be included under the larger umbrella of agencies for the overseas corporation or company. Under certain very restricted circumstances the overseas company will be allowed to have its own branch company in Iraq, if the object or the field in which it is going to operate is of a special technical nature.

Question

Where can more information be obtained about the Arab boycott rule? Is there a publication available in London?

Answer

The best way is to establish contact with the Arab League Office in London, where they normally have lists from which it should be possible to see whether the company is boycotted or not. If it is, further enquiries should be made to find out more about whether the boycott has been lifted or to discuss the possibility of having such boycott removed. Often the name may be included in the list but after about, say, a year or so, it is removed from the list. It is best to keep constant watch.

Question

Host governments habitually guarantee availability of foreign exchange to cover dividends and repatriation of capital, but a clear guarantee of foreign exchange for import of essential raw material is seldom, if ever, available, unless linked to export performance. Is there any long-term formula which can be negotiated prior to investment, and, if so, with which government department: the Ministry of Industry or the Ministry of Finance?

Answer

The easy answer to that question is no. But obviously it depends on where the company is situated. It is a practical matter. The area, as a whole, is not one that is likely to be short of foreign exchange in the immediate future, although there are individual countries that do control the situation very tightly. In countries having this control, such as Egypt (where imports are, in fact, controlled strictly by the allocation of foreign exchange) the foreign companies are probably better off using the free zone where the problem is not relevant.

In Syria, similarly, foreign exchange is controlled very tightly, but there the company is either trading with one of the five government import houses, or, again, is in a free zone. The private import sector is extremely small and the joint venture situation is not really going to arise. The same situation is, to some extent, likely to apply in Libya, where the government position is that all companies in Libya are entirely Libyan owned, so the question of importing, again, by joint venture, should not really arise. In other countries, on the whole, there is going to be no problem about obtaining foreign exchange because there is no apparent shortage of money at present and this is likely to be so for the conceivable future.

Question

On the question of appropriately worded arbitration clauses, is it enough to say that disputes will be solved according to the rules of the International Chamber of Commerce in Paris?

Answer

With regard to all contracts with individuals or companies in the area it would be advisable to have as comprehensive an arbitration clause as possible without conflicting with the rules affecting the local arbitration laws. So the best course would be to consider what the law affecting arbitration is in the local country and then to make detailed principles of procedure embodied in the clause itself and be bound by this. Referring the arbitration to some other international body is becoming less and less acceptable and it is almost invariably rejected if it concerns two individuals or two companies and does not involve the government as a party.

Question

After an arbitration award has been made, do local courts readily enforce it, particularly in cases when the parties have voluntarily entered into an arbitration agreement?

Answer

It is not quite known outside the Arab world that full recognition is given to any provision agreed by the two parties. There is a basic principle in the area which is very much revered in fact, and that is that any contract between two parties *is* the law between them. Thus, as any provision relating to arbitration is arrived at by the free will of both parties, it will normally be found that full recognition is afforded to this, including the enforcement, which is normally embodied in the civil or commercial code of the country. Most civil codes, when they touch on arbitration, stipulate that the decision of the arbitrator or the arbitration panel, or whatever, will be final.

Question

Is there a different word in Arabic for 'agent' and 'distributor', and what are the words, so that they can be easily recognised? Is it possible to avoid the necessity of paying a compensation, if the agency is cancelled by providing in the contract that foreign law applies and that compensation is expressly excluded?

Answer

This is really a difficult question. By law there are three acceptable words—accepted universally in the area, for 'agent'. The first is 'Wakil', which is an exact translation of the word 'agent'. Normally, it is the only word used in the Arabic language. The second—the distributor—is the 'Muazá', or 'agent for distribution'. It does not mean an agent, but it means a distributor. He is not, however, an agent in the sense that the word is used in the English language; he is in fact a man who is the instrument of distribution.

The word 'agent' is becoming less and less acceptable in the area and in at least one country, say in Egypt, it is not possible for a person now to be an agent of an overseas company. So a new term was introduced. It sounds a lot more respectable, but in practice it is exactly the same. This is the 'technical representative'. So overseas companies should have a technical representative—somebody like a consultant—who will work, not by commission, like the agent, but by exact remuneration, or a monthly salary, repaid by that company.

The third term is 'Mumathel'—the nearest translation would be 'representative'. By the way, the word 'mumathel' is a general word—it has no special field of operation and so a Member of Parliament is a mumathel, because he 'represents' other people. If a company send somebody as a proxy, he will be 'mumathel' and if the company has a representative in the area acting on its behalf he is also 'mumathel'. This wide application should be kept in mind, because sometimes when people come across it they think it is restricted to the question of commercial representation.

The difficulties in discussing an agent vary a great deal from one country to another. The difficulties in Iraq will not be the same as those encountered in certain Gulf States. In Lebanon the contract will basically govern the relationship with the agent, but the position is more restrictive in certain countries than in others. However, it is suggested that in the area there is no special tendency to strengthen the position of the agent as against the overseas company. The idea is to preserve his rights as a party to a contract and not as a privileged person in a commercial deal. And therefore, quite often, the agency agreement itself will be the ultimate instrument by which his services may be terminated. Again, what was said above with regard to contracts generally will apply here as well. If the contract is comprehensive enough to cover the various aspects of the relationship with the agent, there is normally more protection afforded than in the case of a generally worded contract, which risks incurring argument and probably interference by the local court to introduce some safeguards for the agent. Comprehensiveness is really the key.

Question

What is the importance of the roles played by local Chambers of Commerce?

Answer

It is normally going to be necessary for companies—whether by way of joint venture, or for trading purposes—to become members of local Chambers of Commerce. This is particularly true in, say, the Emirates. In practice it is going to be the local Chamber of Commerce that is responsible for making the company fall in line with regard to local practices and so on. In Dubai it is necessary for the foreigner in business to join the Chamber of Commerce.

Appendix A

TAX CONSIDERATIONS IN THE MIDDLE EAST

I.—COMPANY INCOME TAX RATES

Note.—Rates are given for general comparative information and may not reflect recent changes in the law in the various countries.

	Type		*Rate*
IRAN	Income:		
	Company tax		10%
	Municipal tax		3%
	Chamber of Commerce tax		0·35%
	Retained earnings:		
	Tax on retained earnings		22%–55%
	Dividends paid:		
	Withholding tax on dividends paid to Iranian shareholders		15%
	Withholding tax on dividends paid to foreign shareholders		15%–60%
	Capital gains:		
	Treated as ordinary income		
	Withholding:		
	Professional fees		5%
	Contracts for construction, etc.		5½%
	*Royalties	paid to foreign firms	15%–60%
	*Management fees	paid to foreign firms	15%–60%

*Normally only 50% is subject to withholding.

	Type	Rate
LEBANON	Income:	
	Company tax	5%–42%
	Municipal tax	15% of company tax
	Reconstruction tax	3% of company tax
	Surtax	5% of company tax
	Retained earnings:	
	No tax on invested capital	
	Dividends paid:	
	No tax is withheld on dividends	
	Capital gains:	
	General capital gains tax	10%
	Municipal tax	15% of capital gains tax
	Real estate capital gains tax	3%–15%
	Withholding:	
	Interest	10%
	Royalty payments to non-residents	10%
	Management fees and technical services	5%
EGYPT	Income:	
	Company tax	17%
	Municipal tax	2·55%
	Defence tax	10·5%
	National security tax	8%
	Total corporate tax rate	38·05%
	Dividends paid:	
	Withholding on dividends	38·05%
	Capital gains:	
	Treated as ordinary income	
	Withholding:	
	*Royalties	38·05%
	*Management fees	38·05%

*Open to negotiation.

	Type	*Rate*
IRAQ	Income:	
	Company tax	15%–60%
	Surcharge	20% on company tax
	Dividends paid:	
	No tax is withheld on dividends and dividends are deductible in arriving at taxable income	
KUWAIT	Income:	
	Company tax	5%–55%
	Dividends paid:	
	No tax is withheld on dividends	
	Withholding:	
	No tax is withheld but royalties and interest are not deductible in arriving at taxable income	
SAUDI ARABIA	Income:	
	Company tax on foreign companies	25%–45%
	Dividends paid:	
	No withholding on dividends	
SYRIA	Income:	
	Company tax	6%–36%
	Surcharge	5% of company tax
	Defence tax	15% of company tax
	Retained earnings:	
	No tax on invested capital	
	Dividends paid:	
	No withholding on dividends	

II.—COMPARISON OF EFFECTIVE TAX RATES

The tax liability is calculated for a company in receipt of taxable income of £500,000 in each country.

It is assumed that the Company distributes £200,000 of its income.

Where appropriate it is assumed that the income is distributed equally to:

(i) a company which is resident in a non-treaty country;

(ii) residents of the Middle East country.

IRAN (R157 = £1)

		R	£
Taxable income		78,500,000	500,000
Company tax—10%		(7,850,000)	(50,000)
Municipality and other tax—3·35%		(2,629,750)	(16,750)
Net income after taxes		68,020,250	433,250
Gross dividend		31,400,000	200,000
Withholding tax on dividend paid to foreign shareholder			
R15m @ 31%	R4,650,000		
R·7m @ 45%	315,000		
		4,965,000	31,624
Withholding tax on dividend paid to local shareholders			
R15·7m @ 15%		2,355,000	15,000
Tax on undistributed profits			
R20m @ 25%	R5,000,000		
R16,620,250 @ 30%	4,986,075	9,986,075	63,606
Total taxes		27,785,825	176,980
Effective tax rate		35·4%	35·4%

Note 1. A company with taxable income of R400m (£2,547,771) with a gross dividend of R150m (£955,414) split in the same way would have a total tax bill of R185,850,000 (£1,183,757) an effective rate of 53·1%.

Note 2. It is assumed that the company is 50% foreign owned and that its shares are not quoted on The Stock Exchange.

LEBANON (LL5·25 = £1)

	LL	£
Taxable income	2,625,000	500,000
Company tax	1,038,450	197,800
Surtax (5% of tax)	51,922	9,890
Municipal tax (15% of tax)	155,767	29,670
Reconstruction tax (3% of tax)	31,153	5,934
	1,277,292	243,294
Effective tax rate	48·7%	48·7%
Gross dividend	1,050,000	200,000

No tax withheld on dividend

EGYPT (E£0·913 = £1)

		E£	£
Taxable income before dividend		456,500	500,000
Gross dividend		(182,600)	(200,000)
Taxable income		273,900	300,000
Company tax	(17%)	46,563	51,000
Municipal tax	(2·55%)	6,984	7,650
Defence tax	(10·5%)	28,759	31,500
National security tax	(8%)	21,912	24,000
Withholding tax on dividend E£182,600 @ 38·05%		69,479	76,100
Total taxes		173,697	190,250
Effective rate		38·05%	38·05%

KUWAIT (KD·675 = £1)

		KD	£
Taxable income		337,500	500,000
Company tax:			
KD300,000	85,949		
37,500 @ 45%	16,875	102,824	152,332
Effective rate		30·5%	30·5%
Gross dividend		135,000	200,000

No withholding on dividend

IRAQ (ID·625 = £1)

		ID	£
Taxable income before dividend		312,500	500,000
Gross dividend		(125,000)	(200,000)
Taxable income		187,500	300,000
*Company tax:			
ID 12,000	4,150		
175,500 @ 55%	96,525	100,675	161,080
Surcharge on tax	20%	20,135	32,216
Total taxes		120,810	193,296
Effective rate		38·7%	38·7%

No withholding on dividend

*Assumes industrial 'limited' company

SAUDI ARABIA (R8·17 = £1)

		R	£
Taxable income		4,085,000	500,000
Company tax:			
R1,000,000	365,000		
3,085,000 @ 45%	1,388,250	1,753,250	214,596
Effective rate		42·9%	42·9%
Gross dividend		1,634,000	200,000

No tax withheld on dividend

SYRIA (S£8·57 = £1)

		S£	£
Taxable income		4,285,000	500,000
Company tax:			
S£ 750,000	215,460		
S£3,535,000 @ 36%	1,272,600		
		1,488,060	173,636
Effective rate		34·7%	34·7%
Gross dividend		1,714,000	200,000

No tax withheld on dividend

Appendix B

INDUSTRIAL PROPERTY, TRADE AND INVESTMENT

SOME KEY FACTORS

	Industrial Property Protection				
	Patent Rights	*Trade Marks*	*Convention Details*	*Address of Government Office*	*Consent for Foreign Establishment*
Arab Republic of Egypt	15 years or 10 if food or pharmaceutical	1st applicant entitled 10 year renewals	International Union	101 Kasr El-Ainy Street, Cairo	A foreign supplier must appoint an Egyptian agent
Bahrain	Only U.K. patents may be registered	U.K. marks registered	None	Registry of Patents and Trade Marks P.O. Box 477, Manama	Usually local agents. Registration at Registry of Commerce
Iran	Up to 20 years. May be by importation. Work within 5 years	10 year renewals. Contestable by prior user	International Union	Edareye Sabte Sheikathah va Mulikiate Sanate Ave., Sabte Kol No. 3, Teheran	Use a local agent
Iraq	15 years. May be importation work within 2 years	15 year renewals must be used. Only assignable with business	None	Director General Registration and Supervision of Companies, Ministry of Commerce, Baghdad	Foreign company may have a branch but may not act as an agent
Jordan	16 years Foreign priority possible	14 year renewals. Only assignable with business	None	The Registry of Patents. The Ministry of Economy, Amman	Foreign Business Control Regulation 1974. Government consent required (exceptions)
Kuwait	15 years	10 year renewals. Prior use objections	None	Ministry of Commerce, P.O. Box 2944, Kuwait	No branch possible. Agents must be Kuwaiti
Lebanon	16 years	Limit of 60 years	International Union	Bureau de Protection de la Propriété Commerciale, Beirut	Registration only
Libya	15 years Work within 3 years	10 year renewals 1st applicant entitled Removal on non-use	None	Ministry of National Economy Bureau for Protection of Industrial Property, Tripoli	Agents must be Libyans
Oman	None. Notices of ownership published	None. Notices of ownership published	None	Ministry of Development, P.O. Box 550, Muscat	Agencies must have 35% Omani participation
Quatar	None	None	None	Ministry of Economic Affairs Doha	Agents must be nationals. If no local agent import may be stopped
Saudi Arabia	None. Notices of ownership published	15 year renewals	None	Ministry of Commerce and Industry, Jedda	Agents must be Saudi Nationals
Syria	Socialised economy		None	Ministry of Economy and Foreign Trade Damascus	Not normally possible trade with State import houses
United Arab Emirates	None	None	None	Ministry of Economy and Commerce, P.O. Box 901, Abu Dhabi	25% of profits to local partner. Deposit if £10,000 guarantee

The address of The World Industrial Property Organisation is:
32 Chemin des Colombettes, Geneva.
Telephone: (22) 346300

Factors Affecting Trading and Direct Investment					Special Factors
Import Controls	*Control on Foreign Investment*	*Remittances*		*Government Supervision of Contracts*	
		Dividends	*Royalties*		
Pay foreign Exchange Allocation to end user	Property—Nationals only. Companies—Law of 9th June 1974 approval	Only possible where initial arrangements authorised		Yes—Law of 9th June 1974	Arabic labels
Certificate of Origin only	Property—Nationals only. Companies—50%	No restrictions		Yes. Arrangements must be equitable	
Authorised list otherwise permits or prohibition	60% Iranian licencing of capital importation and company formation	Subject to consent and exchange availability Accounts must be produced	Contract must be approved	Yes	Copyright only where first publication in Iran
Agents are licenced	Majority local participation. Law 31 of 1957	Subject to Exchange Control approval		Yes	
Licences available subject to Exchange Control	Ministry approval usually required 51% Jordanian	Central Bank Control		In practice	Capital repatriation only after 2 years and in instalments
Generally free	Must be 51% Kuwaiti. Normally Kuwaiti Board	No controls	No controls	Licenced by Industrial Development Committee	25% of employees Kuwaiti
Minimal	Approval of property purchase. Majority of Board to be Lebanese	No controls	No controls	Only where tax exemptions apply	Declaration as to employment of Lebanese
Licencing	All companies must be wholly owned by Libyans	Exchange Control permits are required		Registration of contracts	Local insurance of imports
Few. Duty only at 2%	35% local participation. Consent from General Development Organisation	No controls	No controls	Control of Economic Development Projects	Permits for foreign personnel
Few. Duty only at 10%	51% Quatari ownership of companies. Property—Quatari only	No controls	No controls	Licensing of companies	
Few. Duty up to 22%	In practice companies must be 25% Saudi. Modern company law	No controls	No controls	Licence from Foreign Investment Committee	75% Saudi labour, 51% of the pay-roll
Any private imports require advance deposit	Only possible in free zones	Only possible from free zones	Uncon-trolled if from State company	State companies	
Few	Companies only formed by charter which is discretionary	No controls	No controls	No	Federal structure—local variations

Index

NOTES

NOTES

NOTES

NOTES

NOTES

NOTES

NOTES

NOTES

NOTES

NOTES

NOTES

NOTES